RECIPE
FOR
SERVICE

Tony Johnson

Published by

TheTonyJohnson, LLC
TheTonyJohnson.com

Printed in the United States of America

Cover Design by

ISBN: 978-0-9863912-0-0

Disclaimer:
The purpose of this book is entrainment and education. The author and publisher shall have neither liability nor responsibility for anyone with respect to any loss or damage caused, directly or indirectly, by the information contained in this book.

Contents

Recipe For Service

How to Inspire and Deliver Great Customer Service

Written by
TONY JOHNSON

"There is a Difference Between knowing what great
Customer Service is and DELIVERING IT!"
—TONY JOHNSON—

Published By
THE TONY JOHNSON, LLC

WWW.THETONYJOHNSON.COM

Dedication

I want to thank my wife Melissa for her support
and love. Without her my dream to make this book
a reality would never have become possible.

I also want to thank my Father, Tom, my little Sister, Kristine,
and my Aunt Reta for always being there throughout
the good times and bad. There is something comforting
about having such a great family to depend upon.

I also dedicate this to the memory of my late
mother, Alice. Rest in peace Mom.

I am also blessed with an amazing extended family—
Mike, Michelle, Sue, Josh, Jen, Angie, Shaun, and
Lindsay—Thanks for welcoming us to the family.

To Ben—I am so proud of you!

I have been so fortunate over the years to work with a talented
and diverse group of individuals who have always inspired me
to be a better Leader. It has been an amazing journey over the
years and I was very fortunate to have Leaders early in my career
such as Rick and Mark who made me the Leader I am today. I
was also inspired by my colleagues, mentors, Customers, and
Clients to always put the Guest at the center of everything.
They taught me that was the only way to be successful.

I also want to thank my great friend Geno for always being there.

And finally, to Mario I say thank you for the coaching,
Leadership, and Friendship. You have inspired me!

I want to help you deliver the **BEST POSSIBLE** Customer Service!

Please take advantage of the additional resources beyond the pages of this book.

Customer service takes dedication, focus, and constant attention to be successful. On my website you will find many additional **FREE** resources such as my weekly blog and quick Customer Service videos to help inspire you and your teams to absolutely amaze your Customers.

You can always find me for extra Customer Service Magic and MOTIVATION at:

WWW.THETONYJOHNSON.COM

Feel free to reach out to me or my assistant directly:

Tony@TheTonyJohnson.com

Melissa@TheTonyJohnson.com

I am also available to speak to your group or organization. If you need a high energy trainer for your next event or conference, reach out directly at:

Info@TheTonyJohnson.com

Dates are booking fast, so please call TODAY to add **Motivation, Customer Focus**, and **High Energy** to your Event!

Tony Johnson

A Quick Note Before We Jump In

I know you will find amazing inspiration within this book to really drive great service.

But this is only the beginning of our journey.

Delivering fantastic Customer service takes focus and force of will. In these pages you will take the journey of service excellence which begins by putting the Customer at the center of what you do each and every day.

I am so thankful that you have decided to take this journey together. You probably have heard much about the art and science of customer service to this point, and I am proud that you have chosen to add these tools to your repertoire.

There is nothing that can substitute for a genuine love of people and the Customers you serve. Taking the time to understand them all as individuals and really empathizing with their wants and needs will serve you well.

Too often, we get so busy with the spreadsheets and directives that our jobs often demand that we lose sight of the real reason we are there. Customers are who pay our salaries and the salaries of our teams, as well as guarantee return to your stockholders and stakeholders. This is no small contribution to be sure.

As you read through these pages, please take the time to consider how you can apply these ideas and techniques in your daily work life. This is not meant to be dealt with as theory, but rather to really impact the way you deliver for your Customers.

If you take that time to find the applicability for your Customers specifically and work hard to deliver on those commitments, you'll find yourself with a clientele that is not only thrilled with your service but extremely loyal as well.

I look forward to taking this journey together.

Now let's get started.

Tony Johnson

Recipe For Service

INTRODUCTION

"Try not. Do. . . or do not. There is no try."

Yoda

Some folks would argue that the days of wonderful service have come and gone. As we Twitter, Facebook, and Google away, conducting business on a daily basis becomes less and less personal.

A case could be made, as in the paradox of the world growing larger and smaller simultaneously, that the need for great customer service is more important than ever. That as we spend our days being "social" with friends we have never met face-to-face, the simple act of dining out, going to the grocery store, or enjoying a day at an amusement park takes on new meaning. While we might have found ways to pay at the pump, order our Christmas gifts online, or take in a movie on Netflix®, some things just can't be done on the World Wide Web. And that means that the stakes are higher than ever when we have live interactions with our clients and customers.

I want to begin with a story—I feel like most of what is wonderful and abysmal about guest service can be summed up with simple anecdotes. I think they resonate in a way that nothing else can, and the best part is that everyone has a story about customer service—some great. . . and others, well, not so much.

In 2011, I was flying back from a meeting in Philadelphia and after several delays and a switch of flights, I managed to land in Lexington, KY at about midnight on a Wednesday. This was only a few hours later than my original arrival time, and the joy of not being stuck at a bad airport hotel had washed away any nasty thoughts I had regarding my airline.

And then I headed to baggage claim. . .

I honestly wasn't even all that upset when my bag wasn't there—to be honest I had figured it would be on my original flight which ended up arriving the following day. I tried to check with the airline folks, but as they don't staff their counter after 10:00 pm, I decided to drive the hour and a half home and deal with it in the morning.

So far, I was utterly convinced that I had handled this like a seasoned travel veteran, and was inwardly congratulating myself for the maturity I had shown so far.

Now, little did I know that I was about to be tested even further.

When I called the Delayed Baggage Department, I was in a pretty darned good mood. I might have been a little frustrated that there was no direct line to the airport, but I really didn't want to tarnish my good behavior. And then they answered and it all went wrong.

"Good Afternoon, thank you for calling Baggage Delay this is (Name withheld to protect the innocent). . . How May I help you," answered the call center Associate.

"Hi, my luggage was missing when I landed and I would like to see about getting it located and sent to me," I supplied helpfully.

"Sure, I can help with that—what is your claim number?" He asked.

"I don't have one, but I do have my tracking number from my checked bag," I replied.

"Sir, when you filed your claim with the missing baggage department at the airport they should have given you a claim number for tracking purposes."

"I understand that," I answered, "but they were closed when I landed so I drove home."

"Oh, sir, you must file a claim in person for your lost bags"

"But there was no one there to help me and you don't staff the counter after 10 pm? Was I supposed to sleep there until the morning shift started?"

"Sir, I don't know about your sleeping habits, but I cannot file a claim over the phone. You have to do so in person. You will have to drive to the airport and file it there," he said.

"But that is an hour away and. . ."

"I understand, sir," Replied my new buddy, "But that is the policy."

"So let me understand this," I clarified. "I couldn't file a claim because no one was working the counter, the luggage was lost because you changed my flight but didn't switch my bags, and I'm going to have to drive an hour to the airport to file the claim and get my bag—and you won't do this for me or have the bag delivered to me. Do I have that right?"

"Yes sir, thank you for your understanding."

I hung up the phone and started writing this book. . .

CHAPTER 1
Drive The Experience

Making sure that our customers get the very best products when they visit us is a noble goal. It should be the life blood of what drives our daily business and should penetrate the very core of our institutional conscience.

That said—it isn't enough.

We need to be more than the products we provide. We need to be more than widgets and spreadsheets and chocolate mousse.

We need to be the NASA Custodian.

No, don't close the book. . .

Imagine you are back in the sixties—Camelot, Woodstock, and the space race. The President pushed NASA and the country to put a man on the moon by the end of the decade and the push was on!

Legend has it that President Kennedy was visiting the NASA facilities for the first time when he crossed paths with a janitor. The President introduced himself and asked the custodian what he did for NASA.

Now this is one of those "rubber meets the road" kind of moments. The guy could have said anything. . ." I clean toilets," "I wash windows," or "I sweep floors" would have been very reasonable answers.

"Mr. President, I'm helping put a man on the moon," he replied.

Wow!

That is one of the stories that, regardless of whether or not it is true, has enormous power. The idea of a shared cause and vision can drive an organization in a way which nothing else can. When everyone buys in to the vision and begins to pull the rope in the same direction amazing things can happen. Take, for example, those in the higher education marketplace. When I would speak to groups at colleges and universities—whether they be Dining employees, Student Affairs, or Admissions—we tried to look at the overarching goal of the institution. Some departments were tasked with recruiting and retaining students, others with maximizing their campus experience, and still others with their nutritional and culinary entertainment. But let's face it, each of these departments were ultimately responsible for helping students get a quality education. At the end of the day, if their students don't graduate with a meaningful degree and find gainful employment, nothing else matters much. All the amazing food, community building, and high energy pep rallies are meaningless, if students don't get that sheepskin and find a job to pay back those college loans.

It is the shared vision that makes it work. The commitment is not to the mass of students, but rather each student as an individual. When every staff member on a university campus understands that this is the contract into which they have all entered, magic happens. It inspires that shared vision toward a common goal, which is a very powerful motivator.

The challenge that leaders face is articulating this vision—to not underestimate the capacity of their teams to think big and to be inspired by visionary leadership. Too often, we fall prey to just wanting those darned bathrooms to be clean or the place settings just so or even the grass clipped in a certain way that we forget to share the big picture with our teams. When I hear managers say that their folks won't understand the master plan, it just makes me cringe. Talking down to our folks or not trusting them to buy in to the vision is no way to inspire them—it doesn't challenge them to be better or to strive for the moon, but rather to build silos, while not seeing their impact on institutional goals.

So, it's time to bust through all the nonsense, the clutter, and the noise.

We are living in a world of meaningless corporate speak and jargon—of phrases like "through-put" and "level-setting". The first thing I'm going to ask is that everyone use real words. Now listen, I'm a realist. I understand that every organization has its own flavor, and that sometimes, on the way up the ladder, we all have to embrace the phrase that pays, so to speak, but try to use it like Himalayan sea salt—sparingly and when it can make a difference. The other thing I ask is that when you reach a level where you can speak freely and impact the culture, cut through the shenanigans and use honest language that simply connects the dots and fosters inclusion. Otherwise, we are just perpetuating the problematic nonsense and creating a club that you have to know the secret hand shake to enter.

We are going to talk about speed of service (not through-put), fixing problems (not identifying opportunities), and leading our teams (not level setting).

When it comes to insuring a fantastic experience, the good news is that our Customers are pretty forgiving. They are looking for a level of consistency and professionalism that quite frankly is lacking out there in this world. Consider the popularity of the fast-casual and quick service juggernauts out there; they aren't exactly killing it with their innovation or culinary excellence. I would even go so far as to say sometimes the results are moderately disappointing, but yet folks are happy to continue to visit these establishments and enjoy the fare they provide. I don't want to take a thing in the world away from Applebee's®, Chili's®, McDonald's®, Burger King®, or Subway®—because they have succeeded where so many fail.

They have won at the consistency game. They have found a way to insure that every customer that dines with them has a similar (if not exact) experience every time they visit. Take a minute to think about that—thousands of McDonald's outlets across the United States deliver the classic Big Mac millions of times a year without a piece of lettuce out of place. Now, I know we all have a terrible McDonald's drive through story—the Big Mac was old or cold; they forgot my fries; and darn it, I said DIET Coke! But, put aside the anomalies. And yes, statistically speaking, they are anomalies. When you do so, the modern quick service restaurant is a model of efficiency and consistency, and no matter what segment of the marketplace signs your paycheck, you can learn something.

Apply this model daily in your work life. Take the time to ask yourself how consistent your customers' experience is when they visit your business. Unfortunately, most indicators show that we lose quite often in this arena, but take a walk through the service cycle that your guest might experience and keep detailed notes on your findings. I am sure many will discover that there are pockets that can be tweaked. That's not to say that your organization is doing a rotten job, but rather that there is still room to win.

Look at everything your guest will experience and inspect the consistency of your process.

Does your customer experience lackluster wait times when he or she visits? How can you win here and be ready to redeploy your team to trim those waits?

Do you suffer from inconsistency of service? Is the service fantastic one day and disgusting the next? Are you a hostage to the whims and moods of your front line associates?

How is your cleanliness? It isn't just important for restaurants and hospitals, you know. The way your restrooms and entry ways look is a direct reflection on your attention to detail. The waiting room (along with the restrooms) is typically the first impression folks will have of your business. This is a critical point of differentiation that we will discuss in more detail later.

I was flying through a connecting airport on the way home from a meeting not too long ago, and I was disappointed with the overall cleanliness of the location. In particular, when I went to my gate to check on departure time, I was appalled at the state of the area. The seats were ripped, the windows filthy, there were paper bags and empty cups strewn about the seating area, and a serious amount of trash and debris on the floors. There were more dirty seats than clean, and while I understand that the patrons were the real pigs here, I thought I'd let the gate agents know anyway.

Now I've been flying and working in service for a long time, and I had a pretty good idea about how this was going to go. I honestly tried to approach it with no agenda—just trying to be helpful. I understand that folks are often looking for an angle to get an upgrade or something for free, so I try to be respectful of that dynamic. Coming from the retail business, there isn't a day that goes by when I don't have a guest trying to score some kind of discount—but we can never let ourselves get jaded or we risk missing out on amazing feedback that can help us get better.

So I wasn't surprised when they looked at me with a skeptical eye as I tried to "help" them. I explained how dirty the area was and I asked if they could have someone take care of it. The next thing I know, I was treated to a lecture on how the airport was responsible for the cleaning and the ineptitude of the company with which they had contracted. Honestly, I couldn't have cared less about the inner workings of airport politics—I just wanted a seating area that didn't resemble Times Square on January 2nd. At the end of the day, they tried to pacify me with an upgrade to first class and totally ignored the point.

The point is that perception drives the customer experience. As a customer of an airline, I was never going to blame the airport about the filthy seating area. In my mind that is a direct reflection of the airline on which I was flying. Most customers aren't going to care that you are short staffed on a particular day or that your delivery didn't come in, but rather they are going to see that you let them down that day. Now this may be unfair and may further erode the respect you have for your Customers, but it is the hard truth. So whether it's your fault or not, your Customers are looking to you to fix the issue and make sure their experience is easy and free of hassles. They want you to worry about all the behind the scenes challenges and simply deliver to them a consistent experience that meets their expectations.

If you can do that, you have a far better chance of winning their business and maybe even their loyalty. But for sure, you will win the war for their dollars.

So once your have taken the time to determine how you stack up from a consistency standpoint, the onus is on you to fix it. This is normally where most will discover that there is a breakdown in the process, a gap in the training, or a deficiency in the onboarding.

Many of the principles we are going to discuss throughout this book are going to rely heavily on force of will. For some things, there simply is no silver bullet or cure all. It is about digging in and not taking "No" for an answer. It is about setting the expectation, making sure that the team has the tools and knowledge needed, and then executing the shared vision. This is a time when goals must be set at the highest level and leaders must inspire their teams to succeed. There is no substitute for pushing and pushing and just when the team can't take another thing, finding a way to push even harder. To inspire through words and action to make sure that the goals are met—being the cheerleader, the quarterback, and the referee to emphasize every day the importance of the mission.

It isn't easy, and it isn't fast, but it is possible.

So, take solace in that, as you are putting in the extra hours needed to make your standards the new reality. Know that your constant drive, reinforcement, and recognition can move mountains. But, it can only do so if you stand up straight, look your teams in the eyes, and don't take "No" for an answer. Set those meetings to outline the expectations, own the process, and follow up throughout the change effort. This is about being seen in the business daily, about being a resource and a coach, and about being directly responsible for success. There is one final piece—be sure the team knows you are there for them no matter how successful the change might be. If they understand that if they follow your lead, you are prepared to give away all the credit to them and take all the responsibility for possible failure, then they will be ready to run through fire for you. Why wouldn't they? There is no down side and possibly a huge chance to look like a genius—who wouldn't jump at that?

So, do what is hard. Leave what is easy for those not willing to work as hard. Don't look for the big idea that easily solves the issues—they don't exist. Instead, focus on what is dissatisfying your Customers and driving inconsistency, and then attack it. Put your back into the solution, push hard to make it the norm, and then validate that you don't have any backslide.

Then, it comes time for the fun parts—rewarding your team, enjoying great customer feedback, and growing your business.

CHAPTER 2
The Competition Is Everywhere

"I have been up against tough competition all my life. I wouldn't know how to get along without it."

Walt Disney

The simple truth about the service business is that everyone is your competition. That's a lot of folks with whom to contend, but at the end of the day, the sooner you adopt this axiom the better your will be able to serve your customers. I've spent the better part of my life in the food business, and I am always gob smacked when my colleagues only benchmark themselves against restaurants.

Quite honestly, the competition is everywhere. The next time you are out running errands look at it this way—anyone you are doing business with is your competition. These are the same businesses that your customers and clients are interacting with and they are comparing their experience to the one they had with you last week.

That's right; your dry cleaner is your competition.

Your coffee shop is your competition.

Wal-Mart is your competition.

Amazon.com is your competition.

The call center at AT&T is your competition.

Why?

Think of it like this. . . when folks are waiting in line and being served, they compare it to their experiences with you. Did they receive an authentic greeting? Did they get what they needed? Was the service genuinely friendly? Were they thanked for their business? There aren't a lot of interactions out there that don't need to meet these minimum thresholds to succeed. Even if your business is a call center or online store front, people are still comparing.

Was your site as easy to use as Amazon.com or how did you compare when they last called their bank? Was your billing accurate and the information your team gave correct?

I grew up without the internet at my fingertips every day; I am still surprised and delighted every time I point my URL to Amazon. I know that my son, for example, sees it as just another part of daily life, but I can remember when you had to use a JC Penney or Sears catalog to order something to be shipped to your home. Service Merchandise had a foray into computer ordering in the late eighties with the addition of Silent SAM—a method of ordering that was the natural forbearer to online storefronts. This green screen TRS-80 allowed you to view items in a showroom and then enter your order into the computer. Once you entered your credit card info, you could proceed to the pickup area where your items would slide out of the window connecting the service area and the warehouse facility. While the brand no longer exists, I can remember our regular trips to the mall to shop there.

I remember when the brand went under in the early 2000s, its already precarious financial situation made brand-fatal by the events of 9/11, and waxed sentimental for a moment at its demise. For me, this was the loss of something from my childhood—a reminder of Saturday afternoons out with my parents. This is the kind of emotional connection folks can make with a brand. If you take the time to cultivate these types of relationships with your Customers, they will be more likely to give you their loyalty.

With Amazon, the magic is clear and very similar to what I experienced at age ten with Service Merchandise—as you browse through the available selections you are drawn to the item (and in most cases, items) that will make your life complete. But, it takes the experience to the next level.

Those who shop this site are familiar with what comes next—as you leave to "check out" the site suggests items which you might not have realized you needed but can't live without. Last year, I can remember upgrading my iPad and nearly left without a new cover when the suggestion popped up. I have to admit that, although often this is a little irritating, this time it helped me depart with a great little number that had an integrated Bluetooth keyboard. It is disheartening sometimes that Amazon does a better job of suggestive selling than real, live Associates at the big box stores.

The other thing we can learn from Amazon is their follow up. After you place your order and add the additional items that will make your life complete, you get a "thank you" email in your inbox, along with an order confirmation. Following that, you receive the shipping and tracking information for your packages and estimated arrival dates. Talk about fantastic follow through.

The moral of the story is to keep both your eyes and mind wide open for a better way, and embrace the needs of your Customers to serve them effectively. You don't have to have all the answers yourself, but keeping abreast of trends in trade magazines, the internet, and in the news is a great way to stay ahead of your competition. You may not have time to read all the information out there, but keeping your eye on a few greatest hits will keep you abreast of industry and market trends. Information is easier to find than ever—the trick is not getting side-tracked and picking out the few plums out there from the noise and marketing.

Here are a list of sources you should consider reviewing regularly:

- Industry magazines or newsletters
- Email feeds from sources important to your business
- New York Times business section and front page
- Consumer Price Index (releases monthly from the BLS News Service)
- Unemployment reports
- Disney Institute Blog
- My site complete with videos and posts on relevant Customer Service Trends: WWW.THETONYJOHNSON.COM
- State and Federal governmental bulletins—especially for things like minimum wage and tax rates.

You also learn very quickly in retail that you end up working for everyone who walks through that door. Remember, that great exchange Peter had with the "Bobs" in Office Space:

> **Peter Gibbons:** The thing is, Bob, it's not that I'm lazy; it's that I just don't care.
> **Bob Porter:** Don't... don't care?
> **Peter Gibbons:** It's a problem of motivation, all right? Now if I work my ass off and Initech ships a few extra units, I don't see another dime, so where's the motivation? And here's something else, I have eight different bosses right now.
> **Bob Slydell:** I beg your pardon?
> **Peter Gibbons:** Eight bosses.
> **Bob Slydell:** Eight?
> **Peter Gibbons:** Eight, Bob. So that means that when I make a mistake, I have eight different people coming by to tell me about it. That's my only real motivation is not to be hassled, that and the fear of losing my job. But you know, Bob, that will only make someone work just hard enough not to get fired.

I mention this because the sooner you make your peace with this, the more effective you can be. There is nothing more humbling than having a Customer who insists that they know your business much better than you do. But chances are, if you spend time serving Customers, you will run into someone who has all the answers and isn't bashful about telling you all about it. To which I say, "So what?" Let them tell you. Any chef will tell you that these days there are many who attended the Culinary Institute of Food Network and fancy themselves ready to take on the hot line. They will be happy to critique the meal like they were the judges on a cooking competition and expect the restaurant in question to accept the advice like a gift. Now likely their chief culinary contribution was what they would whip up with cheese doodles and chocolate frosting, but that doesn't mean that the halibut wasn't overcooked.

The key here is to take advice from Customers, determine if it has merit, then put it to good use. If you are getting the same comment from multiple folks, chances are that it's time to put aside your pride and make a change. Be careful to stay open to Customer feedback (remember their perception is your financial reality) but resist the urge to change dramatically from a single comment.

Now, this holds true for all businesses—whether you work in banking, higher education, plumbing, or retail—Your customers are always tallying your performance against others with whom they do business. Again, the internet has allowed for a much more global perspective regarding comparative shopping. A good example of this can be seen in Higher Education. I can remember when I was researching colleges in the early nineties, my knowledge base was limited to whichever Universities I could visit and the brochures I could procure via mail. Now with virtual tours and online information, prospective students are much better informed with regard to their educational choices.

The result is a University culture which is much more in tune to what other institutions are doing. The days of regional dominance by most mid-major universities has ended and they have had to adopt more creative marketing strategies, cast wider recruitment nets, and embrace a more robust definition of service. This adjustment is the same one which brick and mortar store fronts have had to adopt when dealing with online market places. With dwindling enrollment, the competition from online institutions such as University of Phoenix, and a more informed clientele, Universities have had to significantly change to keep up.

The purpose of talking about this isn't to put you on guard for more barbarians at the gate or to give you another target for marketing to attack, but rather to put you on notice to keep your eyes open. I tell my staff daily to keep a look out for great ideas and borrow them—like they say on University campuses: *If you borrow from one, it is plagiarism; if you borrow from many, it is research.*

Black Friday is one of the best places to mine some fantastic ideas. Yes, it's more than just long lines, deep discounts, and a turkey-hangover! Some think of Black Friday as the shopping equivalent of spending time in the Thunderdome. I find it to be a great time to sharpen my service acumen. I share this with you to illustrate how may ideas you can pick up in only a day or a week.

The term was coined during the sixties in Philadelphia in response to the heavy pedestrian and street traffic associated with the day. Later the term would be associated with the time of year when companies would start making money or "get into the black." Regardless of its origin and usage, it is a part of our culture, marking the official beginning to the holiday shopping season.

If you are out during this annual shopping extravaganza, keep your eyes open for those who do a particularly great job here. I personally think that Target, Meijer, Lowes, and Barnes and Noble do very well on this day and during the entire season.

Here are some of the great ideas you should be looking at:

- **Extra Points of Service:** Many retailers are exceptionally busy during the holidays and some win and others lose with their speed of service. Those who win most, often employ additional service points. You may see mobile carts with cash registers or folks employing wireless tablets to check out those with just a few items. At the big-boxes, you'll often see folks at the jewelry counter or lawn and garden areas trolling near the checkout lines for Customers. Often folks forget that there are registers in those areas, so they are underutilized.

- **Managers are Front and Center:** There is no doubt that Leaders should always be out Owning Their Dirt, but you see them, like the Mayor of Retail on Black Friday, out shaking hands, answering questions, and keeping lines flowing. Imagine if they ran their stores that way every day. Powerful!

- **Upcoming Items are Being Previewed:** There is always a sense of wonder during the holidays, and with the New Year right around the corner, "what's next" is always top of mind. Often retailers will be previewing the next big thing to start building excitement for the future.

- **Thankfulness Abounds:** Just like the glut of top ten lists that start to emerge, so does the appreciation. This is always a time when businesses send out holiday cards and New Year's wishes full of thanks and hope. There is never a wrong time of year to say thank you.

These are all fantastic examples of how retailers and businesses crush great service on Black Friday. Now I know it's easy to lament the long lines, hot stores, and rude fellow shoppers, but when you think about the fact that many businesses do over 20% of their annual sales during the holidays, it gives perspective on just how well they do.

So what should you do with all this great info?

- **Take time to thank your Customers**: Not just because it's the holidays, but every day. Many businesses send out thank you cards and give out rewards for being loyal shoppers when the snow starts to fall. That is a practice folks will appreciate year round.
- **Keep that service pressure up every day** just like during the busy seasons. Strive for faster speed of service at check out and continue to train the team to be efficient and courteous at the same time. The idea of those two things being mutually exclusive is a recipe for disaster.
- **Give Customers a sneak peak:** Do you have new ideas and products coming down the pipe? Don't forget the marketing genius of sneak peeks well prior to the official release. Think about how much fun the previews at the movies are when you are catching a flick—this is exactly the same idea.
- **Do something a little Extra that adds a WOW:** For example, if someone asks for directions to a certain department, don't just point, walk them there. This is a step that most won't take which means this can set you apart with very little effort. How great is that?!?
- **Invoke Technology:** Just like retailers utilize mobile technology to improve throughput at the POS, you should be thinking each day how it can improve your Customer's experience. It should never be used just for the sake of

something shiny, but when it can bring real improvement to the experience.

Keep these great ideas in mind during the holidays and well beyond, as this kind of attention can build a solid emotional connection. The end result of this commitment to your brand is consistency, which is the building block of Customer Loyalty, couple that with a commitment to sustain this holiday excellence and make it a part of your service DNA, and your Customers will return for years to come.

So, remember not to pigeonhole yourself—branch out and look at all kinds of businesses. If your customers order from you via the internet, you would be crazy not to use Amazon® or iTunes® or Audible as benchmarks. You can learn so much from the way they do business from their virtual store fronts. Their sites are easy to search, full of information, intuitive in the way they suggest and upsell to your needs, and the way they walk you through the process. When online storefronts mention that those who purchased a certain item purchased complimentary products, it feels more like a value-add than suggestive selling. In other words, if it feels helpful, it's not annoying or intrusive.

How does your business measure up? Always look to train your folks to provide that level of service that can lead to an upsell but not aggravate your customers. It's a fine line, but a profitable one.

I talk to my managers and staff daily about always keeping an eye open for businesses that are getting it right. When you are running errands or heading to work or having dinner, make sure to pay attention to what is going well or not so well.

For example, I always pay attention to how it feels to be in a long line, whether I'm waiting in line at a fast food restaurant, FedEx, or the grocery store. Have you ever noticed that you can tolerate a longer wait to check out when all the registers are being staffed? I find myself very impatient, even with a very short line, when it seems that only one checkout line is open. I think that is why folks rarely voice unhappiness while in line at a sporting venue. They understand that it sort of goes with the territory and if you see everyone pushing their hardest to serve, then you can almost give them a pass for the line and the wait. The key is to be sure that you have everyone firing on all cylinders when you are busy. If your Customers see that folks are lollygagging or playing on their phones while they wait that is definitely a recipe to aggravate them. On the other hand, if you are well prepared, working efficiently, and adequately staffed, your Customers can be pretty forgiving. The other piece is that the product or service has to be worth the wait.

This is something that I think most business fail to recognize. Customers will tolerate a wait. For heaven's sake, look at the wait to ride Test Track, Soarin', or Toy Story Midway Mania at Walt Disney World. On any given day the wait for any of these attractions is two hours or more. Look at the wait to ride The Beast at King's Island—yep, well over an hour most days. Even restaurants can get into the act—walk into a Five Guys Burger and see the pandemonium at high noon.

So why aren't there riots and chaos and unhappy folks? Quality. These experiences, foods, and rides are all something that customers crave—a great thrill ride, a family experience, or an amazing cheeseburger. The finished product is so damned good that folks are fine waiting. They might not be overly thrilled that there is a wait—they might even secretly hate that there is a wait—but they tolerate the wait for what lies at the end. Now the other side of that coin is that the product absolutely needs to deliver.

If the cheeseburger at Five Guys was always dry, over cooked, under dressed, and served on a stale bun we would be having a whole different conversation. But it's not—they do a great job cooking, topping, and sending out the finished product.

As far as the Disney and King's Island rides—folks might bemoan the wait, but they queue back up every time. If Test Track or Soarin' broke down constantly, or if The Beast failed to be an amazing wooden roller coaster, the wait wouldn't be tolerated. But as these attractions are among the most loved in the United States theme park business, it's obvious that they will tolerate a wait if there is a payoff there.

Keep that in mind in your business. Make the product absolutely worth the wait.

The other piece is the sense of urgency. This is where many Customer interactions go south—if people are waiting, then those working customer facing positions have to put the spurs to quick service. That doesn't mean impersonal service. It doesn't mean rushed service. It simply means giving it your all to serve folks quickly and making sure that any and all positions are full during peak periods.

Think about this—you walk into McDonalds®, or your local bank, or Wal-Mart® and the employees seem more intent on talking to each other than talking to you. Frustrating, isn't it? Are you wondering how much faster they could serve you they'd shut up and focus on the task? Don't worry, everyone else is too. Don't give your Customers cause to wonder if you are just going through the motions.

So as you seek to inspire your teams to push for that fantastic service that consistently meets expectation, be sure to focus on quality and urgency. Don't get me wrong, being nice to your customers, smiling wide, and thanking them is at the core of what we should be doing—but so is making sure that they are served a great product in a quick manner.

Focus on those items and you'll find yourself with customers who drive business to you by positive word of mouth and repeat business. That will silence your competition.

CHAPTER 3
The Six Canons Of Customers Service

"One of the deep secrets of life is that all that is really worth doing is what we do for others."

Lewis Carol

No book on customer service would be complete without discussing the basics of what makes up great service. It is up to us as Leaders to be sure that our teams understand this at its most basic level, how to deliver on these principles, and have a grasp of why they are so important.

The best way to be sure that your teams provide great service is to be crystal clear about your expectations. If you don't take the time to communicate clearly, you are leaving the overall experience to chance, and that never ends well for anyone—particularly your Customer.

But this is all by way of saying that providing great Customer service is absolutely your responsibility. Too often Leaders lament at the service their folks give as though they have no power to control it. That is absolutely not "Capital L Leadership." That's minor league thinking that has no place in our recipe for service. To set yourself apart, you have to step up and OWN the Customer experience.

Here are the basics that you have to cover with your teams if you want to drive that amazing customer experience:

SMILE AND WELCOME YOUR CUSTOMER WARMLY

It's easy to dismiss items as too basic to the Guest experience. Resist that urge.

Every list of Customer Service must-dos lists smiling as a necessary piece of the puzzle. Have you noticed how often that isn't delivered in the market place? The fact that this is under-delivered presents fantastic opportunity for differentiation on a field which most think is already well captured. The fact of the matter is that most Customers don't get a smile during their visits and that is where you can steal the show.

There is a lot of discussion around the smile and not a lot of agreement. For my part, I plan to share with you my take on the matter and what I think is important based on 22 years of Customer facing management experience.

First of all, you're not able to not smile back at folks who smile at you, right? Warm smiles make for a fantastic welcome and if you start off an interaction with everyone smiling you're well on your way to excellence. Couple this with a politely phrased greeting and your Customers will feel incredibly welcome.

There is much ado about the psychology of the smile—some say it can make you happier and others say that there is no basis for such a claim. I can tell you that when I'm in the middle of a busy day at work and the business is booming, a smile absolutely makes me feel better. I can feel my heart rate go down, I feel more positive about the situation, and folks smile back which makes me feel good just because. I honestly don't care if it's all in my head or not, because it puts me in a fantastic frame of mind to be "of service." So what do you have to risk? Smile away and let it work its magic.

Now the smile itself isn't enough—it has to be genuine. We've all seen the dead smile—the one that looks better on Caesar Romero or Jack Nicholson than the guy making your burrito. It doesn't quite reach the eyes, you know—now that doesn't make the guy a sociopath, but it doesn't smack of genuine either. This one is tricky because you have to feel it. The best advice I can give is to find your joy. To reach deep down and find the love for what you do and channel that into your daily work—this will make your smile warm and genuine. For Leaders, you don't just have to worry about yourself; you have to help those on your team find the joy as well. This is where those motivational skills will come in handy.

If you started the shift off with a rocking pre-service huddle then you are well on your way. Well placed positive phrases and appreciation will keep you rolling from there. Throughout the shift you'll need to pepper in high energy and well placed recognitions to keep everyone fresh and motivated as the day goes along. It would be great if a dose of positivity at the beginning of the day would carry your team all the way to the finish line, but seldom is that the case.

As for the welcome, well, that's at least a little more straight-forward.

If you've ever walked up to the glowing menu board of a fast food counter and gotten the thousand-yard-stare in return you know why the welcome is so uber important. Nothing says "get away from me" quite so clearly as the blank stare of an uninterested cashier.

But, training can help here. Start during onboarding and set the expectation. From there, you should role play and make sure that your new charge understands exactly what makes for a great greeting. Teach them to stand up straight, look their Guest in the eye, smile warmly and use some equivalent of "May I help you?" The good news is that there are no bonus points for creativity—but there is always extra credit available for hospitality. There are some great examples out there—Chick-fil-A®, Raising Canes®, Lowes®, and Best Buy® are fantastic at the warm welcome.

Once you have the training and expectation squared away, you have to nurture and develop it. If you set the standard and then neglect it, you are just as guilty as the apathetic cashier who sold me my cheeseburger yesterday. You have to train it. You have to model it. You have to enforce it. Otherwise, these are just words with no juice to them.

So take the time to find the joy at work and channel that into a winning smile. You might just find yourself happier, more stress free, and even more productive. But most importantly, it makes you appear warm and friendly to your Customers and those on your team.

This is part and parcel of the mission to ensure that every Customer who visits your business is welcomed as a cherished friend. That can't help but to start each interaction off in the best possible way and begin to drive true loyalty.

PRACTICE FANTASTIC BODY LANGUAGE

No one likes to see Captain Slouchy when they stop by your business. There is serious psychology behind body language, but for most daily interactions the 25 cent version is more than enough to set you apart. There is a lot of information out there on the science of body language—and sometimes it doesn't always agree—but here are some highlights that will definitely help you succeed when engaging with your Customers. The trick here is to not only model these great behaviors but to train and inspire your team to deliver each day.

- *Don't be so serious—laugh and smile with your Customers. This definitely keeps things friendly and upbeat. Of course, if you are having a serious conversation or are engaged in Service Recovery, then you may want to dial down your antics.*
- *Don't cross your arms—it makes you seem closed off. But if you keep an open stance and use appropriate hand gestures you will lend credibility to what you are saying—as long as you don't turn it into the samba.*
- *Stand up straight—don't lean against the wall or on a counter. It is an obvious nod to appearing engaged and ready to serve rather than being bored or apathetic.*
- *Keep your feet and body pointed toward the person you are engaging. It sends a message that they are the center of your attention and you aren't trying to get away.*
- *Keep your chin up and tilt your head slightly—this indicates that you are listening, interested, and engaged.*

- *Maintain good eye contact, but don't stare. Remember, folks don't trust people who won't look them in the eye, but if you stare too deeply, you've become a creep.*
- *Nod during the conversation or interaction to show you are paying attention.*

The most important thing to remember here is not to get hung up on what your body language might be saying—yes it's important, but if you let it eat you up you'll look silly as you try to constantly reinvent your stance to say what you want to say nonverbally. Better to be comfortable in your own skin and find a style that feels "right" to you. That will come through as more genuine than fidgeting for the right posture.

There is also much to be said on the topic of verbal vs nonverbal communication. Albert Mehrabian, a psychology professor at UCLA, crafted the most quoted statistics on this matter. He posited that the breakdown of verbal to nonverbal communication goes something like this:

55%: Body Language
38%: Tone of Voice
7%: Words which are spoken

Those are pretty staggering statistics, and really who knows what the exact breakdown is (and really who cares). The key takeaway is that this is a great stat for shock and awe value and it's not wrong. There is no doubt that when my mom told me that what got me in trouble wasn't what I said, but rather how I said it there was wisdom there. How I wish I'd have listened at age 10!

So long as we understand that there is power in body language and tone of voice, then the research is extremely relevant. And that truly is the intent here—to come to grips with the power of nonverbal communication and to use it to show we care. The first step, as they say, is recognizing the issue at hand and then applying ourselves to improving the situation.

This is another key item to keep at the top of mind during the tours of your business. Owning your dirt is very much about keeping an eye on these executional items. While you are checking to be sure everyone is dressed professionally and wearing their name badges, you should be watching their nonverbal cues. This is a great time to coach in the moment and encourage folks to smile, stand up straight, and engage in a meaningful way. Eventually, this just becomes muscle memory and you will see it in stages become a part of the culture. Remember, though, that the second you stop enforcing the behaviors you desire, there will a slow slide out of alignment.

The best way to ensure that this becomes a part of your team's DNA is to emphasize it during hiring, train it during onboarding, and reinforce through continued coaching as time goes on. Also modeling those behaviors yourself and rewarding those who are role models will give this stickiness with your team. There is a term I want to be sure we all understand—**The Ask**. This is a something you should do. This is a thought or action that can drive results. In essence, this is a call to action to make sure you or your team are executing a core value or activity that will improve your service or leadership.

So let's jump into the first one.

The ask here is clear: Make sure your team is using engaging body language to reinforce the welcoming environment you seek to create for your Customers. It might be something that operates in the background of daily service, but it is no less relevant than a sincere greeting or fantastic product.

TREAT YOUR CUSTOMER AS A CHERISHED FRIEND

This can't just be a slogan—it has to be baked into your DNA.

If you can't put the Customer at the center of your everyday life, then you're sunk. Most businesses ask their teams to do just this—treat Customers well and take great care of them. The reality is often very different as the slogans, training, and expectations fall to the wayside in favor of apathy and lukewarm execution.

This is frustrating at its core because the laminated cards that get posted in break rooms and at time clocks promise a much better reality.

You have to inspire your team to embrace this concept and pay it more than lip service. Here is an exercise which you may find useful to motivate your team. This is something I have used in pre-shift huddles and in training workshops to get folks on the front lines in the right frame of mind.

Ask them close their eyes. Yes, really. Stop rolling your eyes for two minutes and stay with me. By the way, this might not be a bad exercise for leaders as well.

So go ahead, close your eyes. Take a beat. Relax. Now think about the most special person or people in your life. It could be your mom, your sister, your husband, your favorite uncle, your boyfriend, or your kids. Chances are you have that one special person for whom you would move mountains. Now keep them in your mind's eye and ask yourself how you'd like them to be treated when they visit businesses out there in the universe. Better yet, how would you treat them if they stopped into your business?

Chances are you want them to be treated with respect, deference, and hospitality.

So take that feeling. Bottle it. And use it to drive great service. This may sound like a simple exercise, but getting everyone in the right frame of mind to deliver on the promise of great service pays more dividends than you might think. Thinking of folks in your business as cherished friends and not just customers, patrons, or clients will really help you and your team deliver.

Let's face it. Customer Service is something you would expect from a transactional activity. But true hospitality is how we treat guests in our homes or how neighbors treat neighbors. There is powerful juju in those types of thoughts and it can spread as quickly through your organization as the flu in October, if you just give it a push.

The trick here is to not let this dream whither on the cork board along with so many other well-meaning programs.

Just as we have discussed with safety, this has to be something that is nurtured, modeled, and appreciated throughout the day. While there may occasionally be a big WOW, the majority of this effort will be felt in the common, daily interactions that may not be, on their face, all that special. But they are made special by the care taken with each and every Customer. The respect, the genuine caring and the deep desire to please must be felt between the words as the cheeseburger is delivered or the package is prepared for shipping.

The proof will come when you set a fantastic example and model these behaviors yourselves. If you, as a Leader, choose to deliver great care to your Customers, your team will absolutely pick up on that and show them that same love as well.

STAY POSITIVE AND FRIENDLY

Customers absolutely hate negativity!

There is much more power in starting with yes. You would think some days there is a contest out there for how often rules and nonsense can get in the way of a great Customer experience.

Now that isn't to say that you have to honor every single item as requested, but there are ways to satisfy your Customer and "policy" at the same time.

First of all, make sure policies make sense. If it's stupid, then change it. I am sure there was a collective gasp out there by folks who may work for large, corporate entities with lots of red tape. That certainly is a barrier, but not one that should be debilitating. The ask here is to challenge the status quo, to find a better way, and to rock the boat (just a little) for the good of your Customer. You'll have to find your comfort zone with this one, but anything that can satisfy the customer and not break the bank should fall within the guard rails. Of course, engage your Leader for clarity where appropriate to be sure you don't run astray of your organizational mission.

Find a way to use a "why not" rather than a "why" perspective. When we start with YES and move into making that happen rather than finding excuses to say no, this puts us in a frame of mind that leads to solving our Customers' issues. That's not to say that you are going to be able to make an exception to every rule and meet every over-the-top demand, but there is always opportunity to compromise and find a way to creatively address the situation. If you cost your Customer time, is there a way to make that up by moving their order to the front of the line or expediting shipping? If you didn't deliver on a product, can you replace or discount?

Chances are your Customers don't want the world when they ask for exceptions—just to be heard and considered.

The second thing to remember is the need for a positive and friendly attitude. Your Customers couldn't possibly care less about what bums you or your team out—so don't bother them with it.

You can absolutely impact the positivity of your team on a daily basis. If you keep an upbeat attitude and open line of communication with your team, you can absolutely inspire them. Also remember, if you stay positive and friendly with your team then they will pay that forward. Being cognizant of that reflective nature of your team can definitely help you win here.

This is why great Leaders not only stay positive themselves, but are always on the lookout for negativity that can destroy their upbeat mojo. Asking your team about issues they are having, and allowing them to vent about frustrations, can definitely help here. Team members may approach you with personal issues or work based issues, and sometimes all they need is an ear. Taking that time to listen, help with solutions, and **energize them back into position** can help them provide that friendly service your Customers demand.

The same can be said for being friendly. Leaders can inspire this in their teams by making sure that several key actions are clearly defined and scripted:

- **Every Customer receives a warm welcome, including a fantastic smile**
- **Front Line Associates use polite phrases such as "please" and "my pleasure"**
- **Each Customer is THANKED for their business**
- **Only positive phrases are used—and the word "no" is as unwelcome as J.K. Rowling's "He Who Must Not Be Named"**

It is important to note that you can do all of this and things still may not go to plan.

Sometimes you can do everything in your power and folks still won't stand and deliver for your Customers. If you go through a very thorough hiring process, complete with behavior based questions, you should screen out a majority of the Freddy Frowners that we seek to keep off our sales floors. But, solid interviewing isn't foolproof.

You'll have to keep a close eye on your team. The next chapter will teach you how to **Own Your Dirt** every minute of every day to drive results. Manage your shifts minute by minute to be sure that your team is delivering on that promise. You'll have to coach in the moment and follow up afterward on those not making the grade. If you don't take action on those providing less than stellar service, you are endorsing their behaviors by default—and **that poison will quickly spread through your team.**

So the key here is make sure your team understands the service expectation, is empowered to make decisions when it comes to handling Customer requests, and embraces a positive energy.

Sounds easy right?

Well, if it were easy, there would be no challenge. And let's face it then everyone would be able to deliver on these promises and deprive you of the chance to stand apart as the CEO of Service Town.

Take care, stay positive, and head out right now to inspire that positive environment that leads to great service.

Make it Easy

Hassles are such a drag.

Have you ever noticed that some places are more interested in telling you why something can't be done rather than how it can be made possible? It seems like such a waste of energy and a drain on patience. Sure, there are going to be times when you have to say no, but that shouldn't be your default position.

Hassles and inconveniences are huge turn offs to your Customers and in a world which is becoming increasingly complex, you can stand apart if you just keep it simple for folks to do business with you. There is no doubt that the huge WOWs are fun to talk about, and look great in the employee newsletter, but they may not have the impact you wish they did.

The biggest problem with the huge WOW is that Customers are quick to forget the grand gesture or put it in the "feel good moment" file, but it doesn't have stickiness. They are far more likely to abandon a business for poor service and execution than to give their loyalty to a business that provides good service continuously.

Consistency and ease are the big ticket winners here.

Here are some key drivers that your Customers will appreciate:

- **Keep your product consistent.** *I like the lasagna analogy here: if you run a restaurant, it isn't enough to serve delicious lasagna—it has to be the SAME lasagna. Folks want to know that love-it-or-hate-it your lasagna always has mushrooms and Italian sausage. If it is made one way one time and another way the next time, it's confusing and your Customers won't ever know what to think or expect.*
- **Don't make them repeat themselves.** *Customers hate having to tell you and your team the same things over and over again. If they call or engage face-to-face, and you must have another person engage, bring them up to speed first.*
- **Don't overcomplicate things.** *Above all, your Customers are looking for EASY. Don't give them six forms when two will do, don't over-tweak your website, and keep your surveys short. The easier you make things the more likely folks are to come back. That goes for how many clicks it takes to complete a transaction online and how many questions you ask them while you check them out.*
- **Focus on the Opportunities.** *No doubt that you must reinforce positive behavior—and it can give you scalable solutions for your organization—but if things are going wrong you have to focus on them. Schedule meetings designed to shine a light on underperforming segments of your business and devote the brain power of the team to solving them. Take a page out of the Bill Gates playbook and start the meeting off with problems to be solved while everyone is fresh and before you run short on time. Removing obstacles and playing error free ball are much more impactful than pouring energy into service recovery because things went astray.*

Removing obstacles for your Customers should be a key focus for your teams daily. The best way to start here is by understanding hassles that are impacting the Customer experience. You can certainly review your comment cards, analyze surveys, and most importantly ASK THEM. The face to face conversations can certainly yield the best commentary if you take the time to dig deep and listen.

Once you've done your homework:

- *Compile all of the key learnings; then, craft a plan to address and remove the hassles. Involve everyone in this conversation—likely your front line team is well aware of these and probably have some dynamite ideas to solve.*
- *Review the plan with your team to work out these "kinks" in the Customer experience.*
- *Train the team to deliver, both in the classroom and on the front line*
- *Coach your team in the moment to reinforce the training you've given and show that it isn't "flavor of the month"*
- *Codify the behaviors through positive reinforcement and nudging them back on track when they stumble.*
- *Follow up consistently and retrain as needed.*

You have probably embarked on change efforts before and most likely some worked and others didn't. The key is to make sure that you speak the language of convenience whenever you look to add a process or service. Keeping it easy for your customers, and making sure that your teams are well trained to deliver, can yield results when it comes to retaining and growing your Customer base.

And when you tally up the balance sheet, loyalty really means happy Customers that keep coming back.

THANK YOUR CUSTOMER

Sounds so simple, doesn't it?

It might be considered old fashioned, but thanking Customers seems like the least we can do when they pony up hard earned money for our goods and services. Whether you're in banking, cheeseburgers, or widgets, the ask is the same.

When people come into your business be sure you thank them kindly for stopping by.

How often have you left a business without a Thank you? Too often, I'm sure. This can be a huge differentiator—and let's face it, someone plunking down hard earned money to frequent your establishment deserves nothing less.

There is a lot of power behind the thank you—and not just because of the gesture of showing gratitude. Some may see this as a closing, but I see it as an opportunity to start the next interaction. This is a chance to wish your Customers a great rest of their day and invite them back tomorrow. So in a way, you are sowing the seeds of a repeat visit here. This is a chance to make sure they not only know you appreciate their business but to nudge them toward their next visit. You are also closing on a great note that makes them recommend you to their social circles.

So there is thanking and there is THANKING. In lieu of nothing, I'll take the perfunctory gesture, but we all need to strive to be better than that.

1. **Great eye contact is a key.** Just the right amount of eye contact is reassuring and gives an air of authenticity to the gesture.

2. **Smile genuinely.** A smile is a great default position; let that speak volumes about how happy you were that folks stopped by.

3. **Use a friendly tone of voice.** Don't mumble and certainly don't try to be sarcastic. Neither of those things will make your Customer feel sincerely appreciated.

4. **Make the gratitude specific.** Thanks for coming in today. I appreciate you trusting us with your account. You can even deepen the gesture by using your Customer's name.

There is no doubt that as Leaders you likely do this on auto pilot—and probably really well. If not, this is something that practice can easily fix. You have to commit to the gesture and use it liberally. The real impact comes when you have your team in lock step here as well. Many of the folks I see on the front lines in businesses around the country haven't been coached on this and definitely haven't been inspired or held accountable.

The best way to move forward here is to make sure your entire team knows that a sincere thank you is the close to every transaction. They should have the freedom to give it their own flavor and integrate into their customer interactions how they see fit, but it isn't negotiable.

Then you have to validate its happening and coach daily to make sure it continues. Once you get your team in the groove it will be as second nature as those warm welcomes we discussed earlier.

Finally, you can impact this by thanking your team for their good works. Those who feel undervalued and underappreciated are not likely to give away thanks in any great measure themselves. You can also couple this by visiting your team in their work areas and really pumping them up. Not only should you energize them in pre-shift huddles, but throughout the day. Give them warm smiles, ask what they need to better perform their jobs, and remove hassles for them. **With that kind of energy how can they not pay it forward to your Customers?**

So don't leave anything to chance—show your team how it is done, show them you really care, and don't settle for less than heartfelt thanks to your Customers.

CHAPTER 4

Own Your Dirt

"Get a good idea and stay with it. Dog it,
and work at it until it's done right."

Walt Disney

So it's clear that delivering great service, mastering the details, and delivering on the promise of a great experience are crucial to success. That said there is a wide margin between what we all know to be the right thing to do and actually executing on those values and ideas.

So what is the big secret?

The good news is that it isn't as complicated as many make it. It's easy to get bogged down in creating a 287 step plan to Customer engagement and satisfaction. The problem is that the more complicated we make the process, the less the Guest ends up in the center of what we do. It seems to me that we can boil this down to something much simpler.

Two Steps to Inspire Great Service:

1. **Walk Your Dirt**
2. **Repeat until you Own it**

Now that begs the question—what does it mean to own your dirt? Simply put, it's an extension of the management by walking around maxim. Never forget, there is very little leadership happening from behind an office desk. Leadership is a contact sport and begs for in-the-moment management that models the appropriate behaviors. When you own your dirt it gives you the fantastic opportunity to be sure that you are buttoned up in all of your areas. It also gives you the chance to be sure that you are working with your team to make sure everyone is in position at just the right time doing just the right thing.

Using deployment charts to make sure your team is in position is a great way to make sure your dirt is in great shape right from the start. Many businesses with Front Line Associates in rotating shifts don't take the time to be sure everyone knows exactly where he or she will be working. Take the time to detail out the deployment and your team will easily transition from shift to shift. There is a lot of time wasted when the team doesn't know what they are supposed to be doing or when they have to wait to be placed by a manager. The other result is frustrated Associates who could potentially take that out on their Customers—and let's face it, normally your team is at their best when they start, so if you start with them in a bad mood, it's even more difficult to keep them amped up throughout their shift.

Some call this having their aces in their places—I call this owing your dirt. Take the time every day as you walk through your business to be sure that you are constantly looking at how your team is working. There are always ways to be more efficient and more of service to the customer. This is where you can see that Sally's name tag is missing or Jerry could be welcoming Customers more warmly or that Fran never calls for the next person in line to come down to her station (or she doesn't do so very nicely).

Again, this can't happen from your swivel chair.

Having visible leadership on the floor at all times is an expectation that cannot be neglected. This may sound like something that is a given, but if you've ever walked into a business where the managers were tied to their desks, you'll soon see that it is neglected often with terrible consequences.

Being visible in your business—particularly if you have multiple sites which you are leading—can pay dividends in a variety of ways.

It inspires better execution. Actively engaging with your team improves performance, increases employee engagement, and helps turn up the volume on Customer service. All this said, the ultimate goal is to train and inspire your team to provide this high level of service whether you are there or not; but in the beginning, your presence helps develop the muscle memory which leads to great performance.

With few exceptions, the team always executes better when there is a Leader present—its human nature. They stand up straighter, smile more broadly, and often are the best incarnation of themselves in those moments. Think back, didn't we all watch our Ps and Qs more closely when Mom was around?

Spending time out in your dirt makes it so much easier to coach in real time. If some of your associates need additional attention you are right there course correct and give direction. Your team can benefit from in-the-moment coaching but not if you aren't there to do it. There is no better way to reinforce great training than with feedback. Your team is going to need to be nudged back onto course on occasion and the sooner you can do so the less time they have to let poor execution become habit. This is a great way to drive recognition.

You can't catch someone doing something right if you aren't there to see it. So while you are out touring your locations, you have to keep your eyes open for great work that you can reward and celebrate. Just like you must commit to never walk past a problem you also can't breeze by great work. When you see it, say something immediately. It's fine to return later with a card or movie tickets or whatever recognition pieces you use, but the sooner you can appreciate someone the more they will tie it to the achievement you are praising.

It gives you the chance to hear feedback directly from your Customers. Comment cards are great. Surveys are useful. And relayed information from your teams is invaluable. But there is no substitute for looking your Customers in the eye and listening. Plus people sense when you own your space and are willing to listen—and they will reward you with the gift of feedback to help you improve. When you spend time on the front line, it gives you a chance not only to ask direct questions but to listen.

You will hear them talking to each other, making comments to their friends, or even overhear the occasional aside to themselves. When you hear these items you can be right there to fix the issue or make sure they have what they need. Now folks hate a creeper, so be sure you don't come across like an eavesdropping weirdo, but don't ignore someone who is upset or needs assistance.

You can model desired behaviors. When you spend time with your team it gives you the great opportunity to experience front line roles first hand. Take the time to work in these positions, as it gives a great chance to demonstrate your values in real time. You can show your teams that you truly believe in clean locations and great service by actually *doing those things.* The other great payoff here is that by performing front line roles yourself, you can empathize with issues your team may be experiencing and work directly with them to craft solutions. All of this helps you build credibility with your team.

There is so much to be gained when they know you understand what they do each day and that you are willing to pitch in to help out when things are tight. Let's face it, we all have to deal with call offs and empty shifts—there is no better way to help the team get through being short staffed then by jumping in to assist. You can't make it too much of a habit, as then folks may expect it or take it for granted, but if you walk the line here you can really make an impact. Folks will be more willing to adopt new goals and objectives when they know they are coming from a Leadership Team that "gets it."

The key here is commitment. Make time every day to walk your dirt and treat it as the most important part of your day. Put it on your calendar and don't let the other demands on your schedule squeeze it out. Take notes during your visits and when you sit down to summarize your day and plan tomorrow, be sure that you including your findings. If you don't use these as opportunities to drive improvement, you might as well have stayed in your office counting paper clips.

This cannot be undervalued in terms of impact. If you've ever asked yourself why in the heck most folks know what makes up great service but so few deliver on that—this is the reason. There are a lot of talkers out there in terms of driving great service. If you read enough books, attend a seminar or two, or just latch on to principles from successful businesses you can certainly tell a good story. But the proof comes in the delivery.

I can't emphasize the importance of being present in your business enough. You have to walk your dirt daily and make notes. It's fine to set an action plan. It's great to meet with your team. It's amazing to set them with goals to get better. But if you stop there, then you are a manager with a pretty action plan but terrible results. You have to screw down the lid on processes and hold the team accountable for tangible results or you are sunk.

If you are a Leader who also has other Leaders reporting to you, then you must make this important to them as well. If you are responsible for a large operation or multiple sites then you have to rely on your team of Leaders to Own Their Dirt. There is only so much any one person can do in a day—even those who are organized with a great plan and amazing Front Line Associates. You have to depend on your managers to be out on the front line with the team as well. This allows you to not only engage meaningfully with your hourly team but with the Leadership team as well. The more you inspire, encourage, and hold them accountable to be out in the thick of things, the more your service will improve exponentially. The more eyes you have on the operations and Leadership you give to your team, the better the end result will be for your Customers.

This is the big differentiator: The force of will to make things better.

CHAPTER 5
You've Got Your Corporate Training Program. Now What?

"Leadership and Learning are
Indispensable to each other."

John F. Kennedy

The key to making all of these service expectations a reality is great training and Leadership. Most blunders in Customer service are driven by lack of understanding as much as lack of will. Don't get me wrong, you'll encounter your fair share of sourpusses who couldn't find friendly if you drew them a map, but a majority of folks want to do a great job. They just need more training and direction.

If you work for a large corporation, often you are looking to Headquarters or Corporate or Consolidated for your marching orders. That is often one of the best parts about working for a company of size—the robust amount of resources available.

That is a double edged sword to be sure. For every ten great programs or processes you receive, there is one lukewarm meeting-in-a-box that feels absolutely mailed in.

Don't fret, though, as this presents a tremendous opportunity for you as a Leader. I didn't say manager. . . I didn't even say leader with a little "L." I am talking about those of you who are looking to be capital "L" Leaders.

Training programs that aren't very good don't have to be a punishment for your teams. Your company probably isn't in the habit of rolling out programs or trainings for no good reason—if they are, then please find someplace else to work because you are too good for that. But likely there is a legit need—such as a customer service training program.

So let's take that example and run with it. How can you make the most of your company's customer service training program?

Let's start by recognizing that there are companies that do a fantastic job of customer service training and should be proud of what they deliver. If you work for one of those places, then carry on and make great use of these materials. If not, then read on. You picked a great day to stop by.

Often these programs come to the front lines fully baked and ready to roll out. And unfortunately they are often the most vanilla, bloodless programs you are likely to see. They cover the basics and are rolled up in a neat PowerPoint package with facilitator guide and talking points. Finally this program arrives in a Fed Ex box and is dropped on your desk. It clearly states in the roll out memo that this is a mandatory program and it's your job to check the box. So this monster isn't your fault, but it is your problem.

So what do you do now?

Well start by shaking off the notion that this is just a box to check.

You have to find your personal connection to the program and bring the passion. If you don't have any enthusiasm for the information you are sharing, your audience certainly isn't going to either. At a base level, every program is going to cover pretty much the same items: smile, be polite, thank your customers, make great eye contact, suggestive sell, and so on—the trick is to inspire your teams to do this. That is where you can differentiate yourself as a Leader to your organization and as a star to your Customers. This is where your passion will help you win. When you strip away everything else, this is you standing in front of your team asking them to treat your customers well. Much of what they do will be determined by their connection to you, the simplicity of the request, and the example you set long after training ends.

Practice and Rehearse.

In my opinion, 90% of great customer service training is all about the presenter. Does this person make me feel good about what we are discussing; does it make me want to buy in? If you go up in front of the audience cold and rely on the facilitator's guide as a crutch to support you during the presentation, you are cooked before you even get started. When you are in front of your audience, you are a professional presenter regardless of your "day job." Own it and your audience will get engaged. If you want to improve your presentation skills there are books, online videos, and coaches out there who can help you. I'm guessing you know someone in your organization that is great at this, so reach out for help. This person can provide tips and tricks, and might even let you practice with him or her so you can get feedback. There is honestly no substitute for practice if you want to get better. If you want to really hone your craft, work on improvisation speeches. Have you spouse or best friend assign you a random topic, take one minute to prepare then speak for five minutes.

Amp up the content.

Now, I am not advocating for wholesale change of a program you have been tasked to deliver, but can you turn up the volume a little? Can you bring some personal stories into the mix? What about a few fun videos from YouTube to both lighten the mood and drive home a key point? Finally, role playing is invaluable. If you can put your team into mock transactions designed to test their knowledge and let them experiment with what they have learned, you will see their confidence and skill increase.

Keep the information relevant long after training.

If you pull your team in, deliver the content, then never mention it again, it would have been easier to just toss the money and time you spent into the river. It would be just as impactful. Once you thank the team for coming and you hopefully get a nice round of applause, the clock is ticking on the relevance expiration date. Now, you must be sure that you are mentioning the principles discussed every chance you get. If you see someone really living them, then be sure to recognize them for those behaviors. Don't be afraid to plaster these items throughout your employee areas and hand out whatever collateral was provided for reinforcement. If there isn't a small pocket edition of customer service tips provided, then create one. Something, no bigger than a business card, should do the trick—and then encourage your employees to carry them, memorize them, and ask to see them often. You should set a great example and carry one as well. All of this is simply a way to integrate this into your cultural lexicon.

The ask is clear. Don't make your Customer service training just one more thing on your to do list. Take the bones of the program you have been given and add more content. Feel free to use pieces of this book and other key learnings you have acquired over the years to bring to life. You have a wealth of experiences you can add to the content to really add value.

As a Leader it is your job to connect the dots and use personal stories and anecdotes to reinforce. The overall idea of delivering great service can seem complicated and difficult, but you have to make it easy for your team to grab on to these ideals and deliver. Your team, just like your customers, LOVES EASY—so give it to them.

Own it.

Deliver it with passion.

And live those values every day.

CHAPTER 6
You're Only As Good As The Last Experience

"I've learned that mistakes can often be as good a teacher as success."

Jack Welch

I spent a fair amount of time trouble shooting in the retail and restaurant businesses, and there is a saying "You are only as good as your last meal" that is practically dogmatic to those in that line of work. It is pretty common to hear chefs, owners, and managers spout this imperative as if it came down on a clay tablet.

Why do I mention this? Because it's so easy to get lazy when things are going well, but from your Customer's perspective they are judging you daily on your performance.

The fact is that folks are fickle. They have a long memory and will remember that there was a time when your cashier was rude or you opened five minutes late. They tend to remember the negative experiences from the past with amazing clarity but the service wins tend to fade. Some may think that those amazing experiences stick when we go above and beyond—and sometimes that's true—but for better or worse, the negative experiences have more stickiness.

On a daily basis, the thing to remember is that you get a chance to reinvent yourself every time a Customer visits. That doesn't mean you should retool your entire operation or have a frenetic style of service that changes daily, but rather that you can change a Customer's opinion every time they visit. IT can go either way, though—you can change their perception of your business for better or for worse. You can also have ten interactions in a row that rock, but if the last one isn't so great then that will be the one that your Customers have in their mental rolodex when handing out recommendations to friends.

Customers will remember that they love your product or that your weekend staff rocks. But there is a twist—they will also remember when your wash rooms were dirty five years ago or that one time on a busy Friday you didn't have enough cash registers open. The trick is striving for perfect service every time. Now that isn't to say you are going to hit that—and we'll talk about recovering from a service hiccup later—but the goal is what matters. If you push to get it right every time, then if and when you do fall short, you'll find your Customers are more forgiving. They will give you the benefit of the doubt and give you another chance. That's when you have your big opportunity. Pick the ball back up and deliver that same great service they are used to and you have then reformed their opinion. Not that they won't occasionally mention that service failure, but if you handle it well, then chances are that when your Customers discuss your service, the most recent (and amazing) experience will be the one they mention.

So you are probably drawing the conclusion that this idea can be translated to anywhere you meet your Customer. And you would be absolutely correct!

I recall beginning one of my favorite roles at a mid-sized Southern University. I met with some of the development staff to determine just exactly what they wanted from their experience. I find it best when starting a new assignment to get right to the core of things by meeting with my new direct supervisor, clients, and key Customers to find out what success looks like for them. I sat with what seemed to be a very nice assortment of folks who were genuinely concerned about their donors, the financial health of the institution, and the experience they gave to visitors as the front porch of the University.

That being said, the meeting quickly devolved into a laundry list of things we should never do again and would likely be beaten to death for even suggesting. The key here was listening to the positives and negatives from the past—some of which were from the distant past—and then setting their minds at ease that my goal was to deliver what was promised. As I listened to their concerns and expectations, the ask was pretty clear. Work with us to put together a great experience and then deliver what we decided upon. Many of the complaints they voiced came not from things which were terrible—but rather from changes that were made without consultation. They saw it as a bait-and-switch, and it shook their confidence in those who came before me. All they needed to hear was that they would be involved and consulted throughout the process, and that they would be given the service they paid for.

This is something to make sure you are aware of day in and day out. Customers are skittish creatures and will abandon you if you don't deliver. They will find another widget distributor, another restaurant, another car wash, or another bank.

Now the trick here is build up currency—to stockpile ingots of goodwill and partnership. So in a way, you are only as good as all of your past experiences. I'm sure you can relate.

Think about your favorite local eatery. You walk in for a bite and it's always been a place you'd enjoyed visiting. This time, however, maybe you've got a new server or unbeknownst to you, it's the chef's day off. Well, the meal that follows is one that is, well, let's say, lackluster to be polite. The food is slow in coming, its cold, the server has no idea what sauce is served with the fish special—and then there it is. The place has jumped the shark (or hit it's plateau and is now on the downside of it's life cycle). In your mind you have already started to calculate if you are going to give this place another chance, and if so, how many more times you will tolerate such a mess. If you have been going there for years, you might give it another try out of loyalty in hopes that it was just a bad day. If this were your first time, however, chances are you are never coming back.

So think about this daily as you are dealing with your Customers, your clients, your stakeholders. Know that they can have tolerance if you make a mistake—which is good because you will—but if you dip into that well too often you'll find yourself in a very lonely place.

The life span of any business whether it be food, banking, or selling lumber comes right down to the last meal premise. Customers in any line of business are not that different from those heading to the local sit down restaurant for a steak. They have a desired outcome—and it could be a loan, a box of screwdrivers, a video game, or a bottle of scotch—and they are looking to you to deliver. How you fill that need and how much value you impart during the transaction is the rubber meets the road moment that defines relationships.

Knowing your Customer might sound like one of those business clichés that belongs more on a fortune cookie than in an analysis of how to keep your guests happy, but it couldn't possibly be more mission critical. If you know what really turns your Customer on, becoming a part of their DNA is only a matter of time.

How? Thanks for asking—the internet to the rescue.

Most of your Customers have web sites—and most of those web sites have sections that most folks never bother to visits—sections like their guiding principles, core values, and if you really get lucky, a strategic plan. No segment is better at this than large institutions—whether you are talking about hospitals, Universities, or large private sector organizations, they love to tell you what makes them tick. Take advantage of this at every turn and get to know your Customers.

If the Customer has a strategic plan or mission statement this is where you can begin to get into their skin. Let's talk about higher education for a moment. For years, when contractors who have been trying to convince institutions of higher learning to outsource their day to day operations, the tactic was to tell them how they should be doing things and what they needed. This went about as well as you might expect, since no one likes to be told their business by an outsider. Almost every large business or organization can be finicky, change-phobic, fiscally conservative, CYA driven entities. That being said, they are amazing places to work and represent a large market segment to those who service them.

Universities have a long tradition of self-sufficiency—they not only take on the challenge of teaching the next generation of our work force and molding them during a formative part of their lives, but they also take on the task of housing, feeding, entertaining, and cleaning up after all of these blooming minds.

From my 18 year old son to companies with whom you want to connect—no one likes to be told that what they are currently doing is wrong, what they should be doing, or how to do it.

The trick is to take the time to know your Customer—just as we discussed earlier—and find a special way to align. There is no better recipe than listening. Take the time to really understand what your customers are looking for and how you can best deliver it to them. Those strategic plans I mentioned earlier are a great way to get started—they are the roadmaps by which each company seeks to hit their core mission. If you can't find a strategic plan, search the web for their mission statement, vision, principles, or core values. Chances are their CEO's page will be filled with valuable insights there for the reading. This wealth of information is a fantastic way to prepare for a meeting or target your services. Most importantly, if you are doing business with these folks, it will definitely make sure you speak their language and embrace their culture.

This principle applies to all of your Customers. If you run a business that deals more with individuals than companies, then you need to find the best possible way to glean information from your Customers. That can come in many forms, and none of them are particularly complicated . . . it just requires the commitment to get out there and dig for intel.

The trick is to spray to all fields here and utilize all the tools available. Having comment cards within arm's reach is a great start, as is a solid (but very short) online survey. Remember, though, that your baseline research shouldn't be lengthy—and don't use it to get demographic data. If you use 3-5 questions and don't ask for every piece of data you can squeeze out of folks, you will definitely get more participation. Its fine to utilize a longer survey for select customers to get the full range of information needed to be successful, but if you overdue it, you'll find that no one will fill it out.

All of that said there is absolutely no substitute for boots on the ground conversations. If you've ever visited a table service restaurant, you're certainly familiar with the idea of a "table touch."

They are utilized by dining room managers around the country to quickly get feedback on their guests' experiences. These can range from a simple hello and eye contact to a more probing "how was your steak cooked tonight." Regardless of the tactic, the mission is the same—to engage with the customer on a personal level and come away with usable feedback.

This is a tactic which can be used in any service channel. I was at a neighborhood quick oil change location, and the supervisor on duty stopped by to ask how everything was going. That was a first for me (except when they are angling to sell me wiper blades), but I appreciated it. Normally this is a pretty bloodless transaction, but somehow the fact that the manager was checking in with the customers and listening to feedback showed a commitment to improve. And the best part was that I heard this guy come away with some great stuff.

For example, an elderly gentleman commented that he didn't like pulling over the service pit as he was always worried he was going to get off track and end up putting a tire in the service bay. The manager listened until he was done speaking (great listening skills on this guy, by the way), and then told the man with a smile that all he had to do was ask the service technician to drive it into position for him, and he would happily do so while the gentleman waited in the lobby. I thought that was a pretty solid win for everyone.

It's so easy to get caught up in the quest for "Amazing" or "Magical" service. More important is making sure that the basics are well executed

The reason this is worth discussing is that customers don't need that sense of wonder each and every time. What they are looking for first and foremost is to get the service they are seeking, at the price they want to pay, when they need it.

Let's talk about visiting a restaurant for a moment—we all have experience with that. When folks come in for a meal at a neighborhood eatery, they have a very specific set of expectations. If the tables are clean, the food is hot and tasty, and the servers are quick to refill the beverages, then there is a good chance that the diners are going to leave happy. If you throw in a few challenges—dirty tables, cold French fries, or a server who forgets about you because of a large party that just arrived, that will definitely cause problems.

Why?

Because people freak out when something they take for granted doesn't work just right. Think about that for a minute:

- Didn't it tick you off the last time the drive through forgot the ketchup or one of your side dishes?
- What about a loss of power on a clear night for no good reason
- Ever had your cable go dark on the best night of television?
- What about when you can't connect to the internet
- Finally, bad traffic on a weekend when you least expect it

No matter what your business might be, start by looking at exactly what your core customers are looking for—it could be fantastic ice cream; it could be a quick bank transaction; it could be a medical exam; or they might be shopping for paint and lumber. Regardless, if you start by analyzing and scripting what makes up a successful base experience, you can nail that each and every time. Once you've developed that muscle-memory, you can move on to the WOWs.

Any of the amazing businesses you might associate with the "Big Experience" start by getting the basics right. Zappos doesn't abandon on time shipping so they can have fun on the telephone with their callers; Delta doesn't lose your luggage so they can focus on being so friendly; and Disney doesn't serve melted Dole Whips so they can have great fireworks.

If you don't get the basics right, no one will care about the rest.

Remember, start by tackling those base expectations. Don't overcomplicate things or try to move on to those home-run-moments until you have the basics under control. No one wants to do business with folks who haven't mastered their core business, so conquer those daily pieces first and build your customers' trust.

Take the time to listen to your Guests—whether they are individuals or a large company. Use that information to meet their base expectations and deliver the services they want when they want them. If you don't listen and deliver, someone else is more than ready to do so, while they are wooing them away from you.

CHAPTER 7
Delight In The Details

"Quality means doing it right when no one is looking."
Henry Ford

Take care of the little things. It seems like such a simple thing, doesn't it? When it comes to success in the restaurant business I can think of no greater talent of successful chefs and restaurateurs than a fanatic attention to the little things.

It is so easy daily to get bogged down with the big ticket, in your face, squeaky wheel, big hairy problems. When in actuality, the total opposite should be driving you. If you watch the process, if you watch the little things, if you make sure that the minutia is dealt with, the big things fall into place.

A friend of mine used to tell me all the time "I have such arguments with our finance manager. Every time we speak she is drilling me on my product cost, my variance to last year, and how my sales per labor hour are trending. I tell her that I couldn't care less about those things.

"Of course, after the stunned silence she finally asks me 'what the heck do you mean by that?' I calmly tell her that the process matters more to me than the results, because if I get the process right and if we focus on the details, that we will hit our numbers without fail.

"I make sure that our procedures are well written, that we are buying the right products, and that we keep a tight eye on production. I also make sure that we don't risk having a product returned because we cut corners. When I have all those things working correctly, I don't have to care about memorizing or analyzing—everything works out just right."

Wow.

That's the antithesis of how I used to think about things. I was so focused on the result that the process sometimes got lost.

I can't help but gravitate toward Disney for examples of fantastic attention to detail. From the time you enter their resort hotels, you can see the beauty of little things done well. All of their resorts are all themed and whether you are staying at the value All Star Sports Resort or Deluxe Grand Floridian Spa, you are immersed in the story.

If you choose the Polynesian Resort, you'll be treated to a tiki theme to make trader Vic blush. The details of the carved totems, the delicious Char-Sui Pork at O'Hana, and the Kona coffee at The Kona Cafe all lend to the amazing experience. These aren't details that you notice all at once, but each time you do catch a new tidbit, it makes the price you paid for your room worth it.

The Coronado Springs Resort in the Animal Kingdom area of Walt Disney World is another area worth visiting. Themed as a southwestern style retreat, everything from the architecture to the food tells that story. The buildings have the teals, pinks, and yellows you might expect along with roofs that harken back to a Mexican colony. The rooms themselves have Spanish-Colonial style flair, the plants and trees harken of that part of the world, and food drives the experience home. From the Poblano Queso Fondito at the Maya Grill to the Cuban sandwich at Café Rix every restaurant delivers on the experience you would expect from this theme.

Although I'm sure the scene smacks of the "touristy", for me it is a peaceful homage to a beautiful region. There is a lake side watering hole called the Laguna Bar just outside the conference center on this property. It is a little slice of vacation nirvana to grab a beer or mixed drink from the bartender and walk along the manmade lake that stretches through the middle of the resort. On warm July nights you can look across the lake to the rooms on the far side and watch the lights and colors reflect off the water and just feel the stress melt away.

The parks themselves are full of theming and details that absolutely amaze and delight. When you walk through the Main Street of Magic Kingdom and see the period architecture it's hard not to smile. Toss in the smells of popcorn and candy as you walk into the park and you are already immersed in the experience.

And that's what it's all about—the 360 degree experience. That sense of immersion that everyone is looking for in their restaurant, vacation, and coffee shop.

One more Disney example and it comes courtesy of Epcot. If you aren't familiar, the back half of EPCOT is a World Showcase, which is an array of experiences from around the globe. Starting in Mexico with stops in Asia, Morocco, and France along the way, the entire experience is a textbook in detail. The areas use key landmarks such as Big Ben along with music, employees who call those countries home, and cuisine which is as authentic as it is delicious to show their guests (or Guests as Disney would put it) a fantastic time.

The story here revolves around Morocco. When plans for the pavilion were announced, the King of Morocco wanted this area to be the most authentic in the Showcase. To accomplish this, he shared his personal architect with Disney to insure that they were well represented. The area bears the stamp of the King and is an amazing area—it makes you feel as though you are a world globetrotter while you walk through the bazaars and enjoy the performers and cuisine.

And finally, if you want some other fantastic examples, look to the line queues in many of their attractions—Expedition Everest, Hollywood Tower of Terror, Seven Dwarves Mine Train, and Test Track are just a few examples. You can also see these types of details at other locales, such as Universal Studios. The Harry Potter Experiences in their Islands of Adventure are also incredibly detailed and a great example of paying attention to the little things.

I tend to think of Disney as a leader in the immersive experience—they have been doing it since the fifties and honestly, Walt Disney is a hero of mine in terms of putting the customer at the center every day. Anything you watch or read on his process shows that he was firmly rooted in story and detail in everything he did. This won't be the last time I point to Disney as an example—As you may have guessed; I'm a fan and a believer in their model.

But most of us don't run gigantic amusement parks—to which I say, so what!

Take a moment and think about the detail opportunities you might have in your business. As I mentioned before, in the restaurant business there are about a hundred of these kinds of moments before the food even leaves the starting gate.

Think about the parking lot of your business—whether restaurant or not, folks have to find a way into your business, right? If they arrive by car and settle themselves into a space in your parking lot and walk to your front doors, what will they find? Will they find cracked pavement or cigarette butts or faded lines? Will they find the windows to your front door smudged? I know you might be thinking "but I run a bank" or "In the widget business, it's all about the widgets not parking lots," or "I offer a skilled trade such as being a lawyer or doctor so people need my services."

I offer you this: let's say you are a lawyer or doctor for moment. If you are in a knowledge-centric, specialty driven occupation and you still care that your waiting room is clean, your windows spotless, and your signage professional, what does that say about your core duties. That much attention to the little things must show a true dedication to the big stuff. If you can be bothered to make sure there is no gum under your seats and the magazines in your waiting room are from the last couple of months, you have to be one hell of an Optician.

The same is true when you go out to eat. I'm sure you've made these kinds of judgments before. My wife almost always checks out the wash rooms in restaurants before we even order. More than once, we have vacated a restaurant for not passing muster in this department. There is a great Chinese buffet that we stopped frequenting altogether when their facilities consistently fell short. Let's face it, if you walk in and the bathrooms are dirty, tables full of dishes, and the floors are filthy, what is going on in the kitchen. Think about it—but not too long or you'll never go out to eat again.

I can tell you that there is no quick fix to the quandary of making sure the details are fantastic day in and day out. This is where sheer force of will kicks in—the dedication and stick-to-it-iveness to make sure that the little things are just so at all times. There is no magic formula or silver bullet but rather the dedication to not accept anything less than the best.

There are a thousand and one pieces of minutia to monitor.

Let's start with your team. Most likely you already have a code of dress and appearance to which you hold your staff (if not, what are you waiting for?). Your teams should be crisp and well-dressed daily. If you are a coat and tie type of workplace, then make sure that you set the expectation for well pressed suit coats and shiny shoes. If you are a bistro or a grocery store, then make sure the uniform is standardized and your teams don't show up looking like they slept in their uniforms.

If you require name tags (and please, require name tags), make sure the style is appropriate and you hold people accountable for arriving to work with them fixed in place. I challenge you to send them home to get them if they can't be bothered to bring them along. And while we are on the topic of name tags, don't use temporary name tags that you make onsite with a label maker. Take the time and pay a little more money to put folks in a printed name tag. This shows your team that you value them enough to assume they'll be there next week; that you can't simply peel their name off and give it to the next cashier. It's fine to keep some temps in house to make for those who are new or break theirs on the job, but make sure they don't have to wear them for more than a week.

Take the time to look at your business with a critical eye every day. It doesn't take long when you get in a rhythm. Ten to fifteen minutes can be enough to validate that you don't have dusty shelves or plants in your waiting room; it can be enough to make sure the pens at your counters work; it can also be enough to make sure that the floors are clean and shiny throughout the day.

It can also be a great time to make sure that your locations are safe for your employees and your Customers. While you are making sure the floors are clean on a rainy day, you can be sure there aren't any slip hazards, for example. Integrate in a solid safety walk of your business to be sure you aren't endangering anyone who steps foot on your dirt.

Let's talk about Disney again for a minute. They really get it right with their approach to the details and in some cases, the minutia, which makes up their resort experience.

There is one detail at Walt Disney World that really makes an impact—the music. For example, at Coronado Springs you'll find an up tempo beat in the morning as you wander to find your first cup of coffee and a bus to the parks; but in the evenings you'll find something very different. The music is more subdued—slow guitars and fewer drums. This is great for enjoying those lake side cocktails or for a romantic stroll with your spouse.

The parks take the same approach—You won't find It's a Small World playing at midnight at Magic Kingdom, but you won't find slow paced music as you walk into EPCOT at 9 am. They understand that folks arrive at the parks ready to rock, but by the time they reach closing they are a totally different batch of Guests. By 10pm, they have endured tantrums, tears, excitement, whining, and screaming—and that was probably the adults. But regardless of which parks you visit or what time you arrive, you will find the mood, music, and Cast in sync with your day.

So there's a lot to consider here, and it is going to take constant vigilance to make the details sparkle. Folks may not always notice the little things when they are amazing, but they will notice them when they are missing or terrible. Keep in mind that folks aren't going to throw you a parade if you have perfectly clean tables that don't wobble—but if their coffee falls into their laps because the table top tipped, you will certainly hear about it. Chances are folks won't compliment you on your team's clean, professional attire but they will notice if they look like hobos.

There are so many instances where you can excel with the details, but here are few for your consideration:

- Clean windows
- Entry way carpets that are spotless
- Well-manicured and maintained grounds (especially near your entrance)
- No gum under your tables
- Waiting room magazines that are not out of date

- Dust free ceilings and vents
- Clean bathrooms (make sure you have plenty of soap and paper towels)
- Well lit waiting rooms
- Parking lots free of litter and cracked pavement.
- Smudge free walls which are free of cracks and peeling paint
- No hand written signage

Tour your business daily and make sure your team knows how important the details are to you—and you can be sure that they will become important to them as well. If you take the time to look at your business with a critical eye and teach your team to do the same, you'll be pleasantly surprised how quickly everyone can help you win here. Set a great example then hold folks accountable and the mission will be clear. If you accept it, your team will too. For example, if you let your managers put up hand written signs then you are endorsing that behavior. Better to set the policy of typed signage only, make sure the team understands then hold them to it. Keep them in compliance by validating that they adhere to the policy and if you see them deviating, nudge them back on course. If you just tell your team that details matter and then ignore them that sets a terrible example. You have to own the details. You have to love the details. You have to show your team that you won't accept less than amazing details. Anything less than that just says "do whatever you want—I'm all talk."

Commit to be more than just talk—details should be important to you. Even though they may not know it on a conscious level, the details matter to your customers—by paying attention to the little things you will inspire confidence in the big ones.

CHAPTER 8
Innovate To Delight

*"It is not the strongest of the species that
survives, nor the most intelligent,
but the one most responsive to change."*

Charles Darwin

Never forget that innovation is not the key driver to success that many believe it to be. Certainly there are exceptions, but overall solid execution, ease, and consistency wins. Think about the fact that there were several MP3 players before Apple struck big—but they delivered an easy to use product that worked flawlessly. Many of our favorite theme parks borrow from the principles of Walt Disney and the Danish Tivoli Gardens. The point is that being first isn't nearly as amazing as being the best.

Innovation is one of those words that sounds great but doesn't really mean much. I think one of the problems that most plagues us when we try to be creative is the fear of starting. Writers call that the fear of the blank page and artists usually aren't thrilled with a blank canvass.

But the only way to get started is to get started. There has to be a moment when you let go of pride and just dig into coming up with new ideas.

The first thing you have to do is create a safe place that can be used to generate ideas. This stuff can't happen in a vacuum— although every now and again we all have "Eureka" moments. Making brainstorming sessions to be safe places to get ideas out in the open is imperative to generating successful ideas. It has to be okay to have the dumb idea—and it also has to be okay to say that an idea has merit or not. You can break those up into separate sessions for the sake of making folks feel comfortable with sharing. You don't want to have a culture that immediately shoots down ideas, but the reality is we have to get the bad ones out of the way at some point so that we can move on with nurturing those with merit.

You have to encourage participation in these events. It isn't enough to host brainstorming sessions and then have a core group do all the talking. Sure often there are going to be those more willing to contribute than others, but Leaders have to be adept at getting folks to share. There shouldn't be a single person who doesn't have a creative idea to contribute (and if there is, take a closer look at the hiring chapter), so make sure you are getting your money's worth.

It may be uncomfortable for folks to be called upon in meetings to offer up suggestions but if you don't, you will leave ideas undiscussed. I know that may go against the grain of making everyone feel great about whom they are as a person, but a little tension can be a healthy thing. Don't let your team off the hook and remember that it's okay for them to send in ideas after the meeting too. And don't penalize them for having bad ideas—as we said earlier, it's okay for folks to have bad ideas. You don't have to use every idea, but don't make people feel stupid for having one. Often it's not that an idea isn't used that dissuades folks from sharing, but managers who act like jerks when something other than gold is voiced.

This is where it has to be okay for folks to talk to each other. Too often, particularly in large organizations, there is a barrier that keeps folks from communicating—this could be perceived or real, but the effect is the same. When organizations live in silos or make it taboo for different departments to talk, then there will never be the kind of innovation or efficiency that everyone wants.

I can remember working for a large organization with many different divisions, and there was a distinct challenge with communication. In one instance, we had a great candidate who would have been a perfect fit in one of our pieces of business, but she worked under another set of leaders. By the time we sorted out the politics of reporting structure and how to make the request, she had taken a job outside the organization in basically the same role we wanted to promote her to.

This is a classic example of how bureaucracy can debilitate an organization—it makes it sluggish and slow to change. I am happy to say that the organization I mentioned has taken great strides in knocking down communication barriers and silos—but can always be a flatter structure.

That isn't to say that reporting structures aren't important, because they do help reduce chaos, but they can't debilitate creativity. Folks need the permission to communicate and not be bogged down by politics and who reports to whom.

Innovation for your Customers can come in a couple of different forms: There is innovation and change driven by Customer commentary and feedback and there is innovation driven by you. Regardless, you are sunk if you don't listen. There are so many channels to hear your Customers that you should never want for feedback. If you are utilizing comment cards, online surveys, direct conversations, and intercept surveys then you should have a wealth of information from which to draw. I will tell you that no matter how great your comment cards and website might be, there is no substitute for having conversations with your customers. Taking the time to have those quick interactions or even targeting a few key questions has so much more meaning live. The biggest win I believe comes from the chance to ask those follow up questions and dig deeper when you sense there is something there to be mined.

Innovation also requires the permission to make mistakes. There are many companies that are so intent on having the right answer from the beginning that it stifles creativity. There are, of course, risks and expenses when it comes to making mistakes but there are benefits from making them. Many leaders (me included) believe that making mistakes when you are younger really can pay dividends later in your career.

I can remember when I was a young manager and I found myself overextended. I was quick to volunteer for projects and take on added responsibility without making sure that I was buttoned up in my core job. After making mistakes and nearly losing a few key accounts, I wised up to the dangers of overextending yourself. I was lucky to have a leader that let me test my limits with a safety net that wouldn't let me fail. That is what is needed for your team as well.

Make sure that your team has a chance to stretch their legs and try new things. Be sure they have mentors or colleagues that help them develop and will help them learn and grow while still having some supervision. Let them learn new things and cross train in different areas. Not only will that give them perspective in their job, but it will help them find other avenues that they may want to explore as they progress in their career. It will also give you a fresh set of eyes and a new perspective that could lead to breakthroughs and new ideas. Let's face it, we all get that tunnel vision when we come to work in the same space every day and fresh faces always bring new ideas. Now this will lead nowhere if folks don't listen. It is so easy to dismiss new ideas from rookie players—this is ridiculous! Those virgin opinions are often the purest and most motive-free opinions you are likely to get.

The other side of this coin is the knowledge exchange that goes back to the team of the visiting manager. These types of exchanges and development opportunities also impart not just skills but ideas that can be taken back with the Leader when he or she returns to his or her daily assignment. They can't help but leave with open eyes and even more open mind when they finish the rotation.

When you work out these rotations, it's a great chance for your team not only to learn from other Leaders but from the front line as well. Some leaders lose their way during their careers by forgetting what it means to step into a front line role. There is magic in working so closely with Customers and senior Leaders who lose touch are going down a dangerous path. Not only will you become disconnected from those you have committed to serve, but your team will see you as "ivory tower" folks who never get their hands dirty and can't possibly understand what they do.

But when you do work on the front line, shoulder to shoulder with the team, you not only keep your skills sharp and get to hear right from your Customer, but you can glean creativity from the team who probably has some fantastic ideas. The most underutilized resource in most businesses is the front line associate. Don't get me wrong, those brainstorming sessions we discussed earlier are great and all that analytic data you probably get from your marketing group is useful, but there is far more important innovation to be achieved where you meet your Customer.

The final piece here is to remember that every idea won't be amazing right away. Sometimes there are ideas that have to find their way. Great Leaders can see ideas with potential and will push them to be better. Now you will occasionally back a bad horse here, but if you see a inkling of greatness in an idea then let it grow and see what happens. Sometimes a great dish in a restaurant starts off as something lackluster with a seed of greatness. Movies aren't amazing from the first blush of a script. And even amazing destinations like Disneyland needed some time to find their legs. Don't expect more from your team's fledging ideas.

The one thing about giving candid feedback is that it must be timely. Another pitfall that can impact the overall process is the idea of Monday Morning Quarterbacking. The best feedback is that which gives an honest assessment of the idea, coaching to help nurture the idea, and that is given in time to be impactful. Being the type of boss that comes around with the "I Told You So" moment won't endear you to anyone and also will make everyone less likely to take risks and float new thoughts. They will feel like you are waiting in the tall grass to strike when things go wrong, and that is not only terrible for innovation, but will drive your folks away pretty quickly. That could mean disengagement or worse yet, great people jumping ship for organizations that will appreciate their talents and help them cultivate their ideas.

So don't miss out on a chance to encourage your team to be creative and innovate. The real winners are your team who will find themselves contributors to the new ideas and to your Customers who enjoy the benefits of the creativity.

CHAPTER 9
Execute Like You Mean It

*"Whenever I go on a ride, I'm always
thinking of what's wrong with the thing
and how it can be improved."*

Walt Disney

Great Customer service doesn't happen in a vacuum. Of course, it is a huge part of what impacts the overall experience but you have to execute your brand to survive.

Great service can save a bad meal; but a great meal can't make up for bad service. That's true. But the missing words to finish there are "to a point." Your Customers can be very forgiving to be sure—but they are not blessed with great patience. In any business, you only get so many do-overs before your Customers abandon you for someone who doesn't overcharge them, deliver late, or ship to the wrong address. If you execute great service recovery, you can earn a mulligan or two, but if you keep getting it wrong you'll be a nice person with no customers.

So you must emphasize the importance of consistently great execution with your team. They must understand the importance and you have to make your expectation crystal clear. We will discuss training a little later, but your staff must have the tools and training to execute. Too often the reason we run afoul of our Customers from an execution standpoint is because our teams didn't know what in the world they were doing. Letting your team get training at the expense of great service is a dangerous proposition that you should avoid at all costs.

When it comes to execution you can't discount communication. As with great service and listening, most folks know what this looks like—the tough part is translating that into action.

For that, you need a great team.

For a great team, you need fabulous communication.

Communication (or lack thereof) is one of the most mentioned items in a majority of employee engagement surveys. I'll grant you that this is often the catch phrase of the disgruntled employee, but that doesn't mean that it isn't true.

Taking the time to be sure that your teams are ready to deliver on the mission of great service and execution is sure to lead to happy Customers. Most great Leaders with well-functioning teams will tell you that one of the keys to success is well planned and executed team huddles. Running less than ten minutes, these meetings are normally held right before the doors open for the day or at key shift changes to bring everyone together for a quick rundown of the day.

When done well, these short meetings (and you must keep them short), can save you time and keep your team on mission for the entire shift. Unfortunately, these meetings are often neglected or poorly executed, which doesn't do anyone any favors.

Here are some tips to make your next pre-shift a success:

1. **Fight the "there isn't time" Excuse:** That is the battle cry of those who can't be bothered. Unless you are fighting zombie apocalypse there is always time for pre-shift huddles. Bake them into the schedule just like conference calls, employee shifts, and opening duties. They are a part of opening. You wouldn't open without a product or service to deliver, the doors unlocked, or the lights turned on—so why would you open before your team is revved up for a great day?

2. **Keep the Energy high:** "So how is everybody doing this morning?" Hold it. Hold it. That's terrible. That's no way to start a pre-shift. This is a time to energize the staff, motivate them for a fantastic day ahead, and make sure they are all ready to smile and engage. Make great eye contact, smile at

your team, and speak from the heart. Your high energy will be infectious. The trick to being energetic is to be well prepared. If you want to be better at delivering pre-services, then practice.

3. **Stay Positive:** No one wants to start the shift listening to a huge loser who's bringing them down—so don't. Highlight what went well during the last shift, and even spend some time on what didn't go so well. Spin it toward all the amazing possibilities the day holds and how execution can be even better today. That doesn't mean that yesterday was a train wreck just that pushing for improvement gets everyone fired up! If you don't take a positive approach with your team, how can you expect them to be positive with their Customers?

4. **Focus on Passion, Not Facts:** Yes, you have to cover the nitty-gritty stuff—how are your sales trending, what are the organization goals, are there specific targets on widgets for this shift; but that doesn't mean it has to be boring and stuffy. Use this as a time to remind everyone that what you do is amazing and that your Customers are depending on you. Restaurants use this time to review the menu or talk about specials, but whatever you need to cover about your mission that pulls people by the gut will work well here.

5. **Recognize:** Did someone absolutely deliver yesterday? Was there a stand out in the group with regard to safety or cleanliness? Did someone get a great comment from a Customer that you want to share with the team? This is a great place to throw in sincere recognition.

6. **Get Everyone Involved:** Talk less and let your team talk more—now there's a recipe for a great team huddle. Encourage folks to share, and work with them before the shift starts so they can really own it! Audience participation is a must or you are just a yammering bobble head barking out orders.

7. **Don't Neglect Safety:** Safety would normally be first, since nothing—absolutely nothing—trumps safety. But the hard reality is that if we don't pay attention to the first six items,

everyone will be asleep or drinking a big cup of "I couldn't care less." Be sure to highlight the greatest hits—hot buttons in your line of business and any talking points you might have from your Home Office. If you already have a culture of safety, folks should be jockeying to show off the great work in their particular areas.

8. **Begin Leading During the Huddle:** Remind folks of the goal for the shift. How can you tweak your efficiencies; what are your financial goals; are there any new items to share with your customers. If you have areas where you are lagging call them out and discuss how you can utilize your cost-leaders to find savings. This is the perfect time to plant the seeds that will lead to epic service and cost controls.

9. **Don't Skimp on the Customer Service:** We should never practice on the Guest, so this is a great place to talk about removing hassles for your customers. It could be a time to role play or remind folks to smile and engage. Your team wants to do the right thing with Customers, but some need a reminder that they can be a game-changer during every interaction. This is also a fantastic place to remind folks to work clean, keep lines of site orderly, and attack the seating areas to keep them clean and orderly.

10. **Close Strong:** Whether you have a catch phrase, love the high five, or enjoy a rally cry, don't be a lame closer. Keep the energy up right until the end with your signature finish. Send them away hungry for a fantastic shift and amped up for success.

The most important thing to remember is not to neglect these valuable meetings. Create a form or sheet to help guide you at first and keep you organized. Don't let them drag on and never find an excuse to cancel them. If you do them right, your team will be excited for the pre-shift huddle every day.

The other key part of execution is making sure that your processes work and that they all make sense. As I've mentioned before, sometimes you have to take a hard look at how you do things for the good of the Customer experience. I know that we all have a boss, and most likely there are policies, procedures, or guidelines that you are expected to meet for the good of the organization. I further understand that more and more often there is not an invitation to discuss or challenge these regulations as they become more and more prescriptive.

And that is all the more reason to do so!

There is no doubt that most organizations put rules and processes in place for a very good reason. That doesn't mean that they are good for your Customers. So the ask here is pretty straightforward (but don't mistake that for easy).

Ask of every policy: Does this make sense and does it benefit the Customer?

There is no reason to have policies in place that don't make our Customers' experiences better or easier. Honestly, if processes don't meet that litmus test, then those rules need to be changed quickly—unless there is a legitimate risk to safety.

People change policies all the time. Restaurants used to be very rigid about substitutions, special orders, and vegetarian entrees—but things have changed as consumers voted with their wallets. Once upon a time Colleges wouldn't allow students to attend class virtually or rent textbooks. Now a significant percentage of Higher Education takes place online. Finally, airlines once wouldn't dream of letting folks keep their electronic devices on during takeoff and landing. I wrote several parts of this book while taxiing on runways.

So if these areas can make changes, you certainly can as well. Keep a close eye out for policies and procedures that make life easier for the team at the expense of the Customer experience. It could be a return policy or the amount of paperwork for a loyalty program or whether or not you can substitute the onion rings for the fries.

When you run across these types of things, best to examine them closely and engage your Customers and the Front Line to get feedback. Really listen, see what tweaks are needed to make it happen, and what is the financial or human capital impact. Craft your solution and how you will implement the change, then get ready to fight for it. Ultimately, if you answer to a large organization then you will need to take the time to respectfully convince the machine. Sometimes this isn't easy and you won't always win. Make your peace with the fact that you can present a most compelling case and still get shouted down. Take the loss gracefully and live to fight for your Customer another day.

But if you have your change effort well planned out, and if it makes sense, you have a high probability of success. Most organizations aren't in the business of ignoring great, well thought out ideas. If they were, they wouldn't be large organizations. The good news is that every time you simplify a process for your Customer you are moving ever closer to building true loyalty that will stick.

This kind of well managed communication and attention to driving convenience can only benefit the Customer by ensuring that the entire team is in lock step and ready to make things easy.

CHAPTER 10
Hire The Best—Then Train Them!

"Do not hire a man (or woman) who does your work for money, but him (or her) who does it for the love of it."
Henry David Thoreau

The right team on the ground makes all the difference. It is our people who serve, delight, and deliver every day, and without them our Customers would go unserved. They are normally the biggest source of praise and also the most complained about part of most organizations—so the investment in finding and training the best talent cannot be neglected. Having a team that is customer focused and committed to excellence will translate into the consistently amazing experiences we seek to deliver every day.

This is a point that folks make time and again when it comes to hiring. There is no substitute for having fantastic front line associates, supervisors, and Leaders in your organization. But too often when I walk into places I see just the opposite. Let's face it, when you see Captain Slouchy or Bobby I-Can't-Be-Bothered working, don't you have that moment of pause when you think about leaving. Better yet, do you have businesses that if you see a certain someone working that you'll just back out and try again later?

I can totally empathize with that. I can tell you that my bank has one certain teller that I'd rather get sucked though that vacuum thingy in the drive through rather than have to deal with her. There is also a less than hygienic fry cook at a local burger place that has pushed me across the street to their competitors because of his dirty work habits.

This is all by way of saying that having the right team on the ground couldn't be more important. The fact of the matter is that it stinks when you are short-handed. It's easy to fall prey to the warm body syndrome when your team is begging you to hire someone—ANYONE—to fill the void. But this is where you have to be strong and stand your ground.

There is a lot on the line whenever you hire a new associate. You not only want the right person, but you have to consider how expensive it can be. There is not just the cost of placing the ad in the paper or online, but also the training, uniforms, time investment, and effort. Now it's a bargain at three times the price if you get the right person and they rock, but you might as well bet on the horses if you don't take the time to hire the best talent you can.

Now that is really easy to say, I know. But you need to make sure you are doing the best you can to attract and win the best folks.

Start by being a great place to work. Word of mouth is powerful not just for Customers but for those seeking to serve them as well. People know if someplace is rotten or amazing to work. They know if the managers are vested in training, if the pay is fair, and if the conditions are manageable. They also know if you struggle to get payroll done right, if you have a Leader who screams at people, and if you never have the right products for them to do their jobs.

So assuming that you have good street cred and folks actively want to come and work for you, what's next?

1. **Don't panic and hire the first person who walks in the door**. Even if you think they are the right person it is always best to have perspective. I know this sounds dangerous and risky, because you could lose the person. Chances are if you are upfront about your process they'll still be there in a day or two. That said, if you do have THE ONE (all due respect to Neo), then snap him or her up if you're sure—but be prepared to potentially have made a mistake.

2. **Be upfront about the job and the hiring process**. Make sure they know you'll check references, that there is a drug screen that this job involves working with people. Set the expectation that you are looking for folks that will deliver

great service and take care of Customers and what that looks like in practice.

3. **Actually check those references.** It's hard to get people to answer questions these days, but try anyway. Also, if the person is still working at that place, can you visit that establishment? I know many restaurant managers who visit the restaurants of managers and chefs they are recruiting. They aren't going to be any better for you than at their last job—so if they are lackluster there you are hiring mediocrity.

4. **Ask good questions during the interview.** If you stick to yes or no questions you will learn so very little you would have better luck throwing darts at a board to pick your new team member. Ask questions that are open ended and allow for robust answers. Tell me about a time you went above and beyond for a Customer? If a Customer was upset, how would you handle it? What was the best part about your last job? Tell me about a time when things didn't go so well for you and how did you dig out? How do you handle stress? These questions will give you great insight into the candidate.

5. **Let them talk!** I have seen colleagues give job interviews that seemed more about them telling the candidate how great they are than about learning about the person. I am sure you are terrific, but save the chest thumping for another day. Let them expand on their answers, thoroughly explain their ideas, and give you a true sense about who they are as people. Ask questions where it makes sense, take notes if you must, but don't get too wrapped up in mentally composing follow ups—stay in the moment and LISTEN. If there is a little dead air while you decide on a follow up, that's okay. Silence isn't evil.

6. **Use an interview guide.** Making up questions on a fly is a great way to make a terrible hire. Most likely your organization has a guide you can use, but you should add your own flavor to the process by having a few signature questions that help you assess talent. Maybe it's a question that has served you well or one you felt was though provoking from

an interview of your own. The idea here is to find questions that you know will help you make the best choice. It's possible you even have a scoring system—that's great, stick to it and make it work for you. Keep a little room open for the X-Factor, but a solid plan will ensure a thorough process.

7. **Finally, remember that you are seeing this person at their absolute best.** They will never be better groomed, friendlier, more punctual, or better behaved. If you aren't impressed with what you see on job interview day, then you are truly in for disappointment when they punch the clock on their first day of work.

8. **Don't be afraid to take a second look.** I often find that when I write something that I usually think it's the greatest thing ever when it's hot off the presses. When I let it sit overnight and I percolate on it, I often find glaring issues or terrible prose the next day when I reread it. This is the same with candidates. Sometimes 24 hours of thought or a second interview can give you a more accurate picture. Don't be afraid to call them back for a second or third interview and definitely engage the whole team in the process. Have a colleague, supervisor, or even a front line team member interview them. You will likely gain perspective and get a fuller picture of your candidate.

So you can do all of these things and still hire someone who isn't a good fit. It happens to everyone from time to time. But this will substantially mitigate the chances of this happening. So take this seriously and you will see the caliber of your team increase dramatically. You will have Front Line Associates and Leaders who are passionate about service and add tons of value in everything they do.

So then what?

The worst thing that you can do is to hire a fantastic new employee then neglect them. That is the funeral dirge of employee engagement. Chances are you will deflate that great employee or cause them to quit if you don't treat them well and train them immediately. It may seem risky to invest in training as they could leave and take those skills elsewhere. But what if you don't train them and they stick around for 20 years?

When folks start work for the first time you are getting a malleable piece of clay. There is an all start player in there waiting to be developed, nurtured, and turned loose to delight—but there is a long road between day one and Customer Service Rock Star. Michelangelo said that David was in the stone all along; he just had to chip away the extra bits. The same is true with your new team members. They have greatness inside if you can only set it free.

One way NOT to do so is to turn them loose on Customers with no training or substandard training. This is the quickest way to kill the spark of service and take the joy out of the work before the journey even begins. Frustrated Front Line Associates give lousy Customer service and there is no quicker way to frustrate a staff member than to ask them to deliver a service they don't understand.

The first time a cook makes an omelet or an agent opens a new account should not be on a live Customer. The very heart of training is about preparing someone to do a job with confidence, because once you add in the human element of a Customer, there are a million new variables introduced into the mix.

1. **Take care of the basics before your new Associates starts work.** Discuss parking, order keys, set up email, order a PC, and make sure any other needed tools are on hand. Whether it is to equip hammers and screwdrivers or a laptop, be sure that you set them up for success on day one. Not only is it frustrating not to have the tools you need to do your job but from an employer's point of view, do you really want your folks losing productivity while you order the proper tools for them? Always remember that not being properly equipped to succeed and contribute is one of the biggest (and most preventable) employee dissatisfying elements you'll encounter. It is also important to get all the paperwork out of the way early—hopefully you took care of most of this during the pre-hire process along with any background checks, but anything remaining such

as direct deposit or insurance sign up should be knocked out straight away.

2. **Start by setting expectations.** This is a great time to review the employee handbook, discuss service standards, go through the job description, and make sure there is alignment on expectations. Much of this you should already have discussed during the interview process so you don't have a disconnect, but this is a great time to reaffirm. Discuss what great service looks like and how their role fits into the organizational vision. This will help your new team member connect the dots on where they fit in and show them how important they are to the mission.

3. **Orientate them to the organization.** Although you have set your expectations, getting new hires indoctrinated into your organization must be handled with all do speed. Make sure they get a dose of your culture, values, and history to give them perspective. Every organization has a rich history full of great stories and passionate founders—make sure you infuse that throughout your onboarding process. Visual cues from the history of your business along with your mission and values must not only be a part of hiring but included in onboarding as well.

4. **Make sure to take the time to introduce the new team member to his or her coworkers.** Starting work in a new place is scary enough without knowing anyone's name. Just taking the time to make these connections can definitely ease the anxiety of the first day.

5. **On the job training is often necessary—especially for folks baking soufflés or repairing an engine—but this must be done prescriptively.** This is a great way to transfer skills and normally those in these roles are tactile driven on a base level, so this is a welcome way to learn for them. Just resist the urge to throw them into the fire without protection. If you use the classic teach it, show it, and try it model, you have a great chance of success. First, it's necessary to explain the task in detail. There are likely best practices to execute properly, so explain why this procedure is best.

This will cut back on folks trying something different that could be ineffective or dangerous. Next, take the time to model the skill in slow motion while explaining the process. Finally, allow the new staffer to demonstrate the skill under the watchful eye of a skilled coworker. Likely this person will be someone who is trusted to perform this role well and according to the script. It's tempting to stop here and let the person proceed solo—but don't do it. Spend the money, take the time, and let the new team member perform this task several times under the watchful eye of a trainer before allowing them to work on their own. Be sure to ask along the way if they are comfortable with the process and then check in often. These first days are crucial to the long term success of the Associate.

6. **You can't stop with the initial training.** When you on-board your new employees there is always a huge amount of information dumped on them at the outset. Too often this is overwhelming and a hit-and-run type of education. If you can infuse learning into daily work life there will be far more retention. The other key here is continuous education. Regular in-services and trainings are a great way to keep your team on the cutting edge—particularly if you are in an industry that is constantly evolving. Whether you are talking about the Associates on the front line or your Leadership team, you have to continuously develop them. If you and your team aren't learning something each day—and if you as a leader aren't inspiring them to learn—you are on a path to stagnation. This is a surefire way to keep folks sharp. Make your management team better Leaders and keep your Front Line Associates in the know, and they will absolutely be better prepared to serve your Customers well.

7. **Check in regularly on those new hires.** Too often, particularly in large organizations, new hires get forgotten after a few days or weeks. That is, when they get any attention at all and that leads to trouble after the first 30 days. Make it a point to find time for your new team members daily in the beginning then weekly thereafter. Staying in touch

with your team greatly improves their potential for success. Of course, no plan is 100% fool proof—you can follow this entire plan and still have folks washed out.

The key here is not to rush the hiring process and then take great care of folks when they come on board. This may seem like pretty entry level thinking, but you would be shocked at how poorly some organizations do with hiring and training. This is a key source of frustration for employees and it is often top of the list when it comes to comments on employee surveys. Moreover, when you have a talented team that is well trained they deliver great service quickly because they are more engaged and talented. This leads to better Customer satisfaction and a model designed to drive loyalty.

If you want the one thing that can get your Customer service on the right track in a lightening quick manner, it all starts with having the right people in the right roles. This commitment to hiring the best and training them to be amazing will have immediate and sustained impact in your Customers' perceptions of your business.

Your Customers will reward this improvement with their wallets through repeat visits, word of mouth, and social media commentary. After all, most amazing and not so amazing Customer experiences are tied to specific people, not products or companies.

CHAPTER 11
Take Fantastic Care Of Your People

*"My main job was developing talent. I was a gardener
providing water and other nourishment. . ."*

Jack Welch

There is no doubt that the greatest resource most businesses have
is their people. They are the face of the company to customers and
have much more interaction with them on a daily basis than many
Leaders. Most customer service complaints and compliments are
normally centered on people and not products—and that is also
one of the biggest reasons that people become loyal to brands and
companies.

So with that in mind, we need to be sure that we are taking
such amazing care of our teams that they, in turn, will delight our
customers. That seems logical, but if you keep your eyes open you
can see examples everyday of folks treating Front Line Associates
with indifference, neglect, and downright rudeness. So the big
question that hits me every time is "what do you think they are
going to do next?" In most cases they aren't going to stand up to
their boss or tell them that they deserve to be treated better. No,
they are going to turn around and take it out on the next customer
that walks into their space.

The part that really makes my jaw drop is when they have
audacity to be surprised or upset that such a thing would happen.
This is action to reaction in a way that Newton could have used to
summarize his findings. Now certainly we all have those customer
service rock stars that turn the other cheek and move right back

into service mode with grace and charm, but they aren't the majority of your work force.

You have to take the time to remember that front line associates are reflective in nature. The way you treat them is the way they will undoubtable treat your customers—which puts you in a fantastic position.

Be nice to your team.

Not because it's good business (which it is) but because it's the right thing to do.

Mistakes are absolutely going to happen; make your peace with it. But unless you have an employee who is making the same mistake over and over again, roll with it and use it as a training moment. Take this hiccup and scale it organizationally so your customers don't have to go through the same issue again and move on. Now there are some circumstances such as theft, belligerence, cursing in the workplace that you have to deal with quickly and definitively; but most of the issues you'll encounter are going to be simple mistakes. You have better things to do than to dwell on it and your employees have better things to do than take a long walk to the wood shed.

Take the time to calmly discuss the issue at hand and make a plan to move forward. Even if it requires discipline because it's a repeat issue, you can still do so kindly. That's not to say that you don't have to be firm, but be human.

As for day-to-day operations, work with the "ask, don't tell" philosophy and things will roll smoothly. It is such a simple philosophy but it works and makes people feel good about their daily tasks.

One of the biggest mistakes to which most managers fall prey is forgetting to recognize. Now I firmly believe that most leaders believe that they are great at recognition and should, themselves, be recognized for amazing recognition. The truth is that most of us are pretty lousy at it.

The problem with that happens most often with recognition is that folks are waiting for the big moment. We have our shiny recognition programs rolled out by the home office and we are just waiting for that huge accomplishment. The problem with that is that it really doesn't work that way. And the bigger problem is that we all know it. We know that most of the recognition-worthy moments are little, sustainable interactions that make all the difference.

That customer that was just served with finesse when their problem was a little outside the norm—that's an opportunity to recognize. That cashier who always makes sure that her station is organized and comes to you whenever the credit card sticker is peeling—try that one. You can even recognize the supervisor who never misses his pre-shift meetings and is always so energetic. The point is that we all know deep down inside that we need to be better—and the great leaders out there have made it a priority to reward and recognize even the little accomplishments daily.

Now I know what you are thinking, but rewarding often doesn't make it less special. Well, it doesn't. It just doesn't. The fact that you are always looking to call out your team for doing a good job just makes it more likely they are going to listen when you have to talk about something that needs improvement. But that's how it is supposed to work—we reward the good stuff and fix that bad. Now this is very easy to say, but only leaders who execute on that mantra will have the success they seek.

The other note here is to NEVER use positive feedback to mitigate a tough conversation. Often leaders tend to finish a tough conversation with something positive so that it doesn't feel so bad. This is both confusing and selfish. First of all, compliment sandwiches taste terrible and secondly they just confuse the issue. Keep your constructive feedback kind, but firm, and don't confuse the issue by trying to make yourself feel better prior to ending the conversation. End with letting them know that you are there to support them and handle positive feedback in a separate conversation so you don't muddle the feedback. In the long run, this is much more impactful to improving performance.

Let's be clear, I am absolutely not saying to make up things to recognize, but if someone's soup is delicious or they have no time clock errors for a month or they always make sure you lobby is beautiful, then don't be afraid to let them know.

Most of the recognitions given are little more than a conversation. You should be quick off the mark to thank folks, because if too much time goes by it loses its impact. Also be aware not everyone likes there recognition the same way. Some people love the public spectacle and others would prefer a quiet moment—as a leader it is your obligation to learn that about your team and act accordingly. Trust me, they'll thank you.

You should also always remember that no one is ever too old or too senior to benefit from recognition. There are many who believe that when you reach a certain level in any organization that recognition is no longer needed. To that I say poppycock—yes, an outdated phrase for an outdated notion. Everyone likes to hear that they did a good job—some more than others, of course, but still the need is there. So keep that with you through your career. Never stop recognizing. Peers should thank peers; CEOs should thanks vice presidents; and VPs should be reaching out to their area managers.

The best part about recognition is that it's contagious. It spreads quickly in the very best way and only leads to more recognition. It inspires that idea of paying it forward and it quickly flows to the front line team who pass it along to their customers.

That's probably the best part of all. When you take the time to treat your staff with respect and thank them when they do well, they let it flow right into their daily work. Our teams are so reflective that how we treat them is how they will treat their teams or their customers. Just as we said above that poorly treated employees often mistreat their guests, the opposite is true for great treatment.

So there's the key. Make time in your schedule for recognition, even if you have to schedule it in your daily planner or online calendar. Hopefully most of it will come organically as you walk through your business but if you don't make it important enough to land on your task list, you may find yourself in your same old habits of failing to recognize.

Development is the last piece of the puzzle. Regardless of job function, most folks love the idea of bettering themselves. Training and development is a scary topic, but that is because it is usually blown up into something more complicated than it is.

You can definitely start small and work up to your ultimate development goal. We covered training in the previous chapter—but this is something different. This is more in the vein of ongoing training to keep your staff on point with new trends or to develop new skills in your front line team and Leaders. Consider for a moment having them shadow another team member or leader—that is a great way to breed cross training and to broaden their perspective. Whether they find a role they'd like to pursue or one they hate, they have learned something.

You can also make sure that they are exposed to new topics or alternate points of view. Do you have a robust lending library? Having copies of Leadership, Customer Service, and trade specific books available for anyone to borrow has little financial impact but can mean a lot to your team. Have them available in standard print, audio book, or even preloaded on a tablet. Chances are you'll have folks who will be grateful for the chance to learn something and appreciative that you took an interest in their learning.

Remember, your teams are incredibly reflective. If you are looking for a sure fire way to improve your overall customer service, treat your front line teams the way you want them to treat your customers. This is a quick change that pays quick dividends. If you treat them well, coach them often, and develop them thoroughly you will find yourself with a staff that takes fantastic care of their customers. And they do it because you took fantastic care of them.

Taking fantastic care of your people also means not letting lackluster employees highjack the day and ruin the great work of your best people. Although we discussed the need to hire and train the best people and then take great care of them, sometimes you have to prune the bushes a bit.

That means that your standards have to be your standards and you must know what you will and won't tolerate. That may not seem particularly magical, but even the very best companies have to manage their teams performance. That doesn't mean that discipline is their default position, but if they have someone not toeing the line, they deal with it.

One of the best ways to keep your team in lockstep with service is to be very clear about expectations from the offset. We discussed this earlier in the hiring chapter and you have to keep preaching the word of your message every day. It has to be baked into your daily meetings and ingrained in such a way that your employees could be asked the question in the shower and spout out the answer without evening thinking.

You also have to be sure that feedback is a regular occurrence. There is no shortage of Leaders who believe that they are giving regular, daily feedback and then have absolutely shocked employees when they sit down for appraisals. Firstly, they likely skip the simple verbal feedback that keeps everyone on the same path and they don't sit down to review performance with their teams regularly enough. That is easily fixed, although it does take some time investment.

Take the time monthly for a ten minute sit down with your Leadership team and set the expectation that they do the same with theirs. You'll find that regular review will keep the organizational and service expectations front of mind and allow you to more easily course correct. Let's face it, folks don't get off the program in leaps and bounds—it happens an inch a day. So if you can nudge them back that inch every day by being visible, giving good feedback and modeling behaviors, then you are likely to avoid the big hairy conversations that come when the train really gets off the tracks.

When you meet with your team, be sure to let them do most of the talking. Sure you have things you want to share and you should make sure you do so, but be sure you are doing a fair bit of listening as well. Your team should have direct input into their development plans and get the chance to tell you how they think they are doing. This is also a great chance to get feedback on how they feel you are leading them and what kind of development opportunities they would like to see. If you include them in building their appraisals and gain a deep understanding of their goals, you will find yourself with folks who are more loyal and invested in their performance.

So remember that both recognition and performance management are two sides of the same coin. Keeping expectations relevant every day and praising those who do a great job will make everyone's life easier. Sometimes that will mean you have to look to give recognition to those who need it most; sometimes you'll need to pep talk Leaders who are stretching into a new role; and sometimes that will even mean discipline to those who simply won't get with your program. It's not fun for sure, but it is necessary as every person who refuses to make great service and execution a priority is poison to the organization.

The key here is default to recognition and constructive feedback as a part of your daily Leadership. Keeping the message positive to your team will be directly paid forward to your Customers though polite, energetic, and delightful service.

CHAPTER 12
Watching Your Lead

"Of all the things I've done, the most vital is coordinating those who work with me and aiming their efforts at a certain goal."

Walt Disney

Never forget that everyone who works for you is watching you for how to behave. There is that inherent responsibility as a leader to model appropriate behavior at all times and to insure that we show the very best of ourselves to those who work with us and for us.

I think this concept might have taken me the longest to grasp. I never really understood how impactful a Leader's behavior can be on his direct reports. I suppose somewhere deep down I figured that I should put a lid on my temper tantrums, but much past that I didn't have a clue.

And then Angel happened. And no, I haven't changed the name—out of respect and a still too raw sense of mourning—I used her real name.

Angel worked for me at a mid-sized University in 2009. We all have those employees who get to us. . . you know, the ones who get into your skin and who just seem so perfectly suited for what they are doing. That was Angel.

Angel was in her mid-twenties and was a lead employee at our Coffee Shop. She was a bubbly and vibrant front line associate who was a poster child for what Coffee Shops try to embody as a brand—she was fast, accurate with orders, appropriately chatty with the guests, suggestively sold, and received glowing recommendations from campus administrators. She had just been accepted to the nursing program and was working to make a huge change in her life. We had worked with her hours and found a way to make everyone happy and it seemed like we were on our way to a great success story.

And then she died.

Yes, she died. I received the news at 3:00 in the morning on a cold Thursday night, and well, it hurt. It hurt like hell. If you've never had a member of your team die, then you can't really understand. It's easy to say that they are a cog in the wheel, or that it's sad and all but after all, it wasn't your wife or sister. But I have to tell you, if you have built that close knit team we all dream about, then it's going to hurt. In the retail and restaurant world, we work a lot of odd hours. Late night and weekends are the norm and it can build a sort of camaraderie that you don't find in 9-5 jobs. Since most of us thrive on the odd hours, lack of sleep, and long shifts, our coworkers are a big part of our core social structure. So, when these kinds of things happen, they tend to hurt even more. And hurt it did.

I was sort of numb as I hung up the phone, and after trading a few texts with some of the team, I realized sleep wasn't an option, so I got ready and headed to work.

I was a little unclear of how to proceed. I remember the cloud that was hanging over the place. This sort of unsaid something as people snuck to the wash room to have a little cry or wiped tears at the time clock, or whispered in shaky voices while they got ready to open.

I thought maybe it would be best to let them work it out on their own. After all, what could I offer that they couldn't give to each other? Would giving it voice make it worse? Would it bring it to the surface and not allow us to get anything done the rest of the day? Surely it was best to let it alone. So I did. I focused on budgets and performance evaluations and preparation for an upcoming meeting. And I couldn't have handled it worse.

Finally, one of our hourly supervisors walked in my office and looked at me.

"Why haven't you said anything to us?" she asked. "Everyone out there is walking around like they died and they don't know what to do. You need to talk to them. You need to talk to us."

Well of course I did—why it hadn't been as obvious as the presentation I was working on eludes me even today. I don't know why I didn't march straight in and do what I eventually did—but I learned a lot about Leadership that day.

I called my client and let him know that I was going to address the team. I had my managers and department heads gather the team and within 15 minutes, I had 100 folks standing in front of me in our largest meeting space. There were tears and there were shell shocked looks—and they were lost.

I cleared my throat, looked them in the eyes, and spoke from my heart. I had taken a few minutes to think about what to say, but for one time in my life I didn't rehearse. I left it raw and unedited and honest. I told them that it was okay to be pissed off; I told them that it was okay to be sad; it was okay to cry. We had lost a member of our family and it wasn't okay. We needed to grieve and we needed to talk about it and we needed to find a way to function. It was going to take a long time to be okay and all we could do was the best we could. We had thousands of people to serve over the next four or five hours and of all people, Angel would want those folks taken care of. She would want us to miss her, she would want us to grieve her, but she would want us to take good care of our Customers and of each other.

I think it could have been one of the best speeches I've ever given. It wasn't the most polished to be sure, but it was the most heart-felt. There were some tears, but there was also the beginning of closure. We took a moment to share some fond memories and then went back to work.

Now was it perfect? No, absolutely not. But it did put a band aid on the wound and allow us to push on with the day. It allowed everyone to open their work areas, count their cash drawers, and serve our Customers.

This was when it hit me. The people who work for us care about what we have to say and what we do. This makes the argument for modeling appropriate behavior crystal clear. Our teams look to us for how to behave; they look to us on how to talk; they look to us to model the correct behavior.

This should both delight and scare you. We've all had "those" bosses. The ones who are hot headed, ill tempered, and difficult to work for.

So here's the deal—do the right thing and always act like your mom is watching. As cliché as that might sound, being a professional is not overrated; watching how you talk to people is important; and you have to treat your folks the way you want them to treat your Customers.

As Leaders you have the power to show your team what matters to you. I have two examples that I often fall back on when talking about this—name tags and trash. Too often when I see organizations that stumble with Customer service, two telltale signs are a lack of consistency with name badges and dirty locations. If you want to get your team's attention here, lead the charge with both!

How often do we see executives who run operations that require their team to wear name tags, yet they act as though they are above such things? Too often. If you want to inspire your team here be sure you wear yours proudly and encourage your team to call anyone out (including you) if they fail to do so.

As far as trash goes, if Leaders won't walk by a scrap of paper on the floor or a dirty lobby then you will definitely show your team how important it is to you. Say what you will, your team does care about what you find important—but only if you show them rather than bark it at them. You can scream about being cleaner, but you'll get much quicker and long-lasting progress if you live that brand.

So embrace your role as a model of great behavior and use it to drive the progress you are seeking for your business.

Be aware, though, that this can go both ways—lose your temper, cut a corner, make an inappropriate or mean comment—that will stick too. Making it crystal clear how you feel with regard to race, sex, age, or decorum by saying and doing the right things will take your team much farther than mere lip service alone.

And I can tell you that it works. When I started a Leadership role with an organization in Chicago, I hadn't become a student of great service yet. We were struggling mightily with engaging our Customers and we needed to repair our reputation of providing lackluster service. After reading a couple of books and doing a little research I caught the service bug. I can remember my boss calling a meeting and spending an entire day discussing how to push our associates to stand and deliver for our customers. We preached and begged and disciplined and didn't see a lot of change. But as our managers and supervisors started to live the message it began to click.

Our leadership team refused to walk past a problem—trash on the floor only required a little dip and scoop; a dirty table just needed a little spritz and wipe; a disheveled employee needed a new uniform and some coaching. And it was looked at as just that simple—it's not complicated to clean a table or pick up a straw wrapper or hand an employee a new name tag—you just have to do it. You have to make that commitment that you won't let something slide as "good enough" and it doesn't matter if the day just started or if it is nearing the end. Quite honestly, if you can't do that then you need to go do something else.

And this doesn't work in just one type of business—this is easily translated into whatever you do. Mechanics shouldn't tolerate disorganized tools or oil all over the floor. If you work in an office don't let the trash cans get too full and for heaven's sake keep the restrooms clean. Regardless of whether or not you are a restaurant, public relations firm, or dentist office please have clean bathrooms. If you don't folks won't come back. If you can't keep the toilets clean you certainly can't be trusted with my tax returns.

That's the real trick—model the behavior you are seeking. As I mentioned with my team in Chicago, it doesn't matter what the task at hand might be—if it's important to the Leaders, it will be important to the Front Line Team.

One thing that must be a Leader's focus daily is safety. This takes real force of will to keep top of mind.

When you ask most businesses what is most important to them, many will come right back with SAFETY.

Of course, that's the responsible answer. That's the answer most feel they are supposed to give. It's the answer that says—profit? No, not us, first, we all have to be safe.

For the most part, I think a majority of the companies and businesses who say that are being honest. They honestly want safety to be the most important thing. Sadly, when the rubber meets the road, most fail to live up to that lofty goal.

Don't take it too hard; it's no one's fault.

> *Safety isn't sexy.*
> *Safety isn't flashy.*
> *Safety isn't marketable.*
> **But Safety IS the most important thing.**

When you walk into a business, you can just feel it, right? You can sense when a company doesn't value safety. Now that doesn't mean that there is a rabid wolverine in the lobby or an active volcano in the parking lot. It's much more subtle than that, but no less noticeable.

It could be the peeling tile in the lobby that is a slip hazard. It could be the wet floor during a rainy day that no one mops. It could be the way you have to exit the parking lot because of an obstructed view or a busy street.

For some businesses, like healthcare, restaurants, and construction firms, safety is critical. In these areas, lapses in safety can result in someone becoming extremely ill or even dying. So in some businesses, safety really is a matter of life and death.

The good news is that with a little time and dedication you can really nail down your safety practices.

It starts by setting policy. You are going to be safe and you are going to clearly define your standards and practices. It doesn't have to be complicated—in fact it should be as simple as it can be. Easier to remember is easier to execute.

Then you have to communicate the vision. Make sure that you take the time to meet with your team to discuss. If you can give your program a great name and market it as heavily internally as you do your product to your customers, that starts to create a culture. Make sure that you reinforce with professional signage and discuss every chance you get. Talk to your team about safety during staff meetings, pre-shift huddles, and performance appraisals. We are talking about the health and safety of people we work with and serve every day—bring the stories home with a personal touch and you'll find they have more stickiness with your folks.

"How would you feel if you didn't take the time to mop the floor and Gladys slipped and fell?" you should ask. By the way,

Gladys is a sweet, grey haired 86 year old widow who is everyone's favorite. She's been your Customer for about 632 years. No one wants Gladys to get hurt.

But seriously, you have to make it personal. You have to find a way to hit your folks in the gut here a little bit so they'll care. Find personal or national stories that will help make your point and make sure you stay engaged and excited about safety. Keeping your team and your Customers safe should have an emotional pull that you can use to drive success here. Commit to live these values yourself and then work hard to set a good example for safety.

It would also be a great practice to have a Safety Team that meets regularly and helps craft policy and evaluate progress. This should be made up of Front Line Associates with one designated as your Safety Captain. This kind of involvement from the front line will help with buy in, and let's face it, peer-to-peer communication is often better received when policy shifts occur.

Finally, you have to recognize great behaviors. When you see someone living your safety culture, make sure they know they are appreciated. It could be movie tickets or a thank you card or a candy bar—but anything quick that can let them know they nailed it will go a long way.

A couple of fantastic things happen as you build this culture. Your team will begin to feel much more valued as you speak the language of safety. They will also begin to police their Leaders, locations, and each other to maintain safe work practices. The great part about this is that valued, engaged Associates give fantastic customer service.

So start by taking a safety walk around your business. From there you can craft your list of items you want to address and put together plans of action to attack. This will become the basis of your daily safety review and your safety checklists. Place a manager or supervisor in charge of the process and check in often to make sure they are well supported and are driving the process forward.

Remember, safety comes in all shapes and sizes—occupational safety, food safety, cash handling security, physical safety—and they all have their own particular pitfalls.

But one thing is certain—Customers won't forgive a lapse in safety. They are forgiving in nature, but no matter how amazing your product might be, they are not likely to remain loyal to a company with bad safety practices.

So it's easy to see that what you do and say matters. You have the power to be a change agent not just for your Customers, but for your team as well. What you say and what you do will become a part of your team's execution lexicon. And that can be for better or for worse.

So what kind of behaviors will you model? This is a great place to make the choice to only show your team your very best self. The trite expression says that a great leader won't ask anything of his or her team that he or she wouldn't do himself or herself. That's a great philosophy. Now turn up the juice on that and you'll be in business. Stop telling your team what to do and start showing them. Lead everyday like you were the star of a training video—are you behaving the way you want your team to behave? If not you're in trouble—but the good news is that it is never too late to start. You have the power to inspire through your actions and show them exactly what good service and execution looks like.

But it's a double edged sword. If you mop the floor spotless with just the right technique or always wear your name tag, chances are your team will pick up on that do the same.

However, if you walk past trash, bad mouth your Customers in the break room, and keep your work area a mess, your team will see that as acceptable.

Your father may have gotten away with that "do as I say not as I do" management style but you certainly cannot. Take the time to determine exactly what is most important to you and then head out into your dirt and set a fantastic example!

CHAPTER 13
Keep It Clean

"The way to get started is to quit talking and begin doing."

Walt Disney

Customers are prone to snap judgments.

They make decisions very quickly when it comes to how they perceive your business and the service you provide. With that in mind, it is critical that each and every part of the customer experience is managed and tweaked to show you in the very best light. Because when things aren't right it can cast a shadow on the mission and product you work so hard to provide.

Cleanliness is a vital part of the overall experience. If you are telling yourself that it doesn't matter in your line of work, then you are fooling yourself. It is most important in restaurants, healthcare, and education, but don't think that folks aren't watching your sanitation basics when they visit.

It could be as simple as your washrooms or the parking lot your guests walk through on the way into your business. If you have dirty bathrooms, cigarette butts on the ground, or dead leaves in your entry way, folks are going to assume that you may not be someone with whom they want to do business. They may not know why right away. . . it could be something that just pulls at their gut. Something that sends out a warning, on a conscious level they may just be thinking that it doesn't feel right doing business in someplace that isn't clean.

But there is much more.

Some folks recognize this on a more unconscious level, but in a nutshell they are asking themselves what is going on that they can't see. When a business disregards the things that are right out in the customer's face, they risk the question of what shenanigans are going on behind closed doors.

Think about it from the point of view of a restaurant visit. If you walk into your neighborhood eatery and the glass in the front doors are in need of a good cleaning you may walk in without much thought. Does the dust on the window ledges in the waiting area give you pause or is it the dirty bathrooms? My guess is that by the time you get the menu, that is more scratch and sniff than anything you are pretty sure you're not eating anything out of that kitchen. If they are so cavalier with all the items they know you can see what do their coolers, stoves, and work tables in the closed kitchen look like?

I don't know about you, but I'm not wasting a weekend with food poisoning to find out.

So think about it carefully and be sure that you are walking your spaces to validate your cleanliness. Utilize cleaning schedules and opening checklists to be sure that there is accountably and process. These can't become "check the box" exercises or there is no point to them. Discuss the expectations in your staff meeting and make sure that you emphasize how personally important this is to you and your guests.

Finally, involve your entire staff in the best way to tackle this challenge and keep the importance top of mind. There is no substitute for an eyes-wide-open approach that sets high expectations for achievement. Make it a contest, give out tons of recognition and praise, and coach through the change with positivity and enthusiasm.

Keep an eye on your cleanliness and it will allow your product and service to shine!

CHAPTER 14
L.E.A.R.N. Service Recovery

"The road to failure is paved with bad service."
Tony Johnson

I love looking for better ways to get the job done. I think that we often learn as much from what isn't working at a particular restaurant or hotel as we do from what is working. If it sucks, fix it. It couldn't possibly be simpler than that—but we've all seen companies get it horribly wrong. Remember that if something goes wrong or isn't working, and you can fix it, there could be gold there.

For example, let me take you back to a New Year's Eve not so long ago. My family and I were dining at a popular eatery in Lexington, Kentucky. The place was your typical white table cloth steak house with a few modern dishes on the menu and an old-school scotch-and-soda-sort-of-feel (but in a good way).

I had only been married about 6 months and I was treating my new bride, her sister and her sister's boyfriend to a nice New Year's Eve meal. Knowing that the other two were your typical poor college students, it seemed like the perfect way to give them something special and score some points with my new bride all at the same time. Needless to say there was a lot riding on this meal.

The restaurant was doing your typical three course dinner with a "choose one item from list A and one from List B" sort of shtick. They started off quite nicely with individual spinach and artichoke dips and a good healthy dose of bourbon.

Course two was not what I would call a rousing success—at least not at first. I remember that my sister-in-law and I ordered the sea bass and it arrived at the table undercooked and cold in the middle. Before you smack me with a bag full of sustainable tilapia for indulging in a fish that would make The Monterey Bay Seafood Watch pass out, remember that it was New Year's Eve and also that this is one darned good tasting fish. Yes, indeed, it seems that endangered fish tastes better—could be the added condiment of fear that makes it so delicious.

Now this was a turning point in the meal—it could have gone one of two ways. We could have had an airline kind of disaster (like I mentioned in the beginning) or something more akin to a Disney moment. Thank goodness, it was the latter.

The server apologized and took the food back to the kitchen, offering to leave the sides to hold us over while we waited. Shortly thereafter, one of the managers stopped by the table to apologize—nice touch, right? That manager, also, gave us an update to let us know that they were close to having our entrees corrected. And finally, one of the chefs from the kitchen came out and apologized just before our entrees arrived. Now here is the part that sealed the deal. The fish arrived perfectly cooked.

It was **service recovery** 101 executed to perfection. So let's talk about that for a moment. Mistakes are going to happen and it comes down to how well those mistakes are handled. The first thing you need to do is let go of the expectation that you are going to be perfect all the time. Strive for it. Ask for it. And expect it. But at the end of the day, you have real live folks working for you and not robots, which is a good thing, because robots are scary! But, with real live, flesh and blood employees you are invariably going to have mistakes made.

Customers are exceedingly kind when it comes to service miscues if you take great care with proper service recovery.

If you follow a few simple steps you can mitigate most service issues that might crop up. Keep in mind the L.E.A.R.N. system—Listen, Empathize, Apologize, Resolve, and Never repeat. Here are the tips you will need to execute amazing Service Recovery:

1. **Listen:** Upset Customer have a lot to say, so best to break out those fabulous listening skills and pay attention. Take

notes, ask questions, but most importantly, **let them talk.** Sometimes it is enough for a Customer to give voice to their displeasure, so resist the urge to interrupt or let your attention wander. They will eventually run out of gas, so hang in there.

2. **Empathize:** True understanding can't be reached unless you take the time to truly look at things from your Customer's point of view. Especially useful here is the idea of repeating back key phrases and internalizing how you would feel if this were happening to you. Often what seems like an irrational request or over-the-top reaction seems much more reasonable when you understand the crux of the dissatisfaction. **This is good place to use your heart as well as your head.**

3. **Apologize:** If you made a mistake, own up and apologize. You can certainly offer to replace the item or correct the mistake if applicable, but often the fix is far simpler than folks make it. Some businesses fail to realize the power of a sincere and heartfelt apology and that it should be specific and never caveated with excuses. Too often folks try the "I am sorry but. . ." approach, not realizing that everything they say after the "but" is irrelevant and seen by the Customer as an excuse. Sometimes just saying you are sorry is enough.

4. **Resolve:** Deliver a product that is executed correctly, apologize once more, and thank the customer for giving you a chance to repair the problem. Keep the guest updated while the item is being fixed, enhanced, or replaced. There is nothing more deflating for a Customer than to go through the trouble of complaining and explaining only to be met with the same substandard execution. Speed here is crucial and the best way to achieve that is by making sure that your team knows exactly what they can do to correct. Make sure they know that they can replace soggy French fries or a toy with a missing piece without prior approval. They should also know how to report the resolution and at what point they need to engage a Leader for approval.

5. **Never Repeat:** When Customers complain, it provides a great opportunity to learn and improve. The key here is not to repeat the same mistakes—Customers are forgiving to a point but they can lose confidence quickly. If you take the time to share these issues organizationally, then everyone can learn from these miscues and improve.

Now here is the part that many folks don't consider. Taking care of an upset or irate customer can be very draining. They can be hateful sometimes and often they will say things that may take you by surprise. Chock that up to an entitled culture that is used to getting their way. Not that they shouldn't expect great service, but often they go well over the line when expressing their discontent.

The important thing here is to be sure that you take some time for yourself. The toll this can take on you mentally cannot be overestimated and you can't let these Customers burn you out. So take a minute, take a breath, and regroup. Maybe you have that best friend at work that can always cheer you up—if so, go find them and let them pump you back up. The power of friendship and camaraderie can definitely help you put some fuel back in the tank for your future Customers. Do whatever it takes to get you service-ready. It might be a breath of fresh air or a quick drink of water—but whatever that might be, do it without delay. The quicker you get yourself back into a great state of mind, the quicker you can get back on the front line and serve your Customers.

Remember, if you don't take the time to regroup and recharge, you will not be able to put your best foot forward for those you will serve next.

Believe it or not, most folks understand that with human beings, mistakes happen. And generally speaking, they are usually pretty forgiving if we own up. It's the folks who can't admit anything went wrong, or even worse, make excuses that lose their Customer's loyalty. I came to the realization a long time ago that no one really cares why things went wrong, but they are very concerned with what you are going to do to fix it and make sure you don't have a repeat performance.

I've always had the best luck with looking an upset customer in the eye and apologizing straight up. I find that a smile in these cases can be disarming and good eye contact gives that impression of trust. Let's face it, do you often trust someone who won't look you in the eyes? We will talk more about body language, facial expressions, and eye contact later but intuitively we all notice these behaviors and respond accordingly—even if we don't think about it.

I remember as a young manager the mistakes I would make when dealing with irate customers. I can remember being a retail manager on a college campus and dealing with an unhappy student customer. I went about it totally the wrong way and then realized too late that listening is the best way to figure out what is going on.

Great service can usually save a bad experience—but bad service, well, no manner of amazing product will resurrect that experience.

The reason I shared the story of my New Year's Eve meal is that now I benchmark service against my experience at Malone's. I look for that level of commitment when I visit Wal-Mart or go to the post office or when I visit another restaurant. More to the point, I look for that level of resolution when I'm out and don't receive great service.

So while you are focusing on playing error free baseball every transaction each day, the reality is that you are going to have issues from time to time. Take solace in the knowledge that your Customers will care more about how they are treated during these issues than about the actual issue itself. If you remember to L.E.A.R.N. during service miscues you can not only correct the mistake but use it to deepen overall Customer loyalty.

CHAPTER 15
Leading the Change

"Change is the law of life. And those who look only to the past or present are certain to miss the future."

John F Kenney

So the toughest part about all these principles and bullet points and lists for success is that they are not a cure all. All the "great service through more pie" or "Zen and the art of customer service" will get you nowhere without force of will.

Since there isn't an easy button to insure success you have to be a dynamic force every day. That means you being the cheerleader, the standard bearer, and the spark plug to make it happen. Sounds like a lot of responsibility—well it is. And this is one of those moments where if you aren't a fan of checking your email late at night or staying half an hour longer because one of your staff is deflated because they've been working a million hours, or something isn't quite right in one of your areas and you need to spend an hour helping your team get it right, then you should go do something else immediately.

Now, I'm not saying that you need to sacrifice your family, social life, and hobbies for the sake of your career. I am saying that you need to be sure you are putting in the hours that it takes to get the job done and lead the change. At first it won't feel like it's worth it. At first you may want to give up. And all of that is okay

We've all been there—leading change is hard and sometimes it doesn't feel all that rewarding when you are in the middle of it. But it's like the analogy of the wilderness explorer leading a group through the forest. He may seem like he is in charge—and to some extent he is—but the person who cut the trail actually formed the guard rails for the mission.

Ask for thoughts about the change effort, but keep the goal in mind. It is easy to believe that you have the very best idea in the world but if you don't allow for input from the team and make sure you have buy in you are sunk. You can unilaterally declare martial law and mandate adherence but while you might see short term success it won't last. The more involved the front line team feels, the more likely they are to be change agents that will help you move your plan forward. Be reasonable, listen to their ideas then plot a course. Be open to divergent points of view and if you hear something worth adding or integrating into your plan, great—if not don't be swayed. Unless you have compelling reasons to make changes, have faith in your plan and inspire your team to get on board.

Discuss with the team the best way to implement the change. As a leader you may have a great global view on the organization and the need for amazing Customer service, but you will need the team to find the best way to implement. After you have taken the time to share your vision with the team this is a great time to enlist their help with implementation. Chances are they are already aware of the issues and likely have great ideas to solve the issue and make your change efforts a success.

Be absolutely clear and open about the change and what it means. This will build trust about the change effort and keep rumor mongering from derailing your process. This means to be transparent about goals and the amount of work expected from the team to achieve the goals. If you don't take the time to honestly share the goals and why they are important, you'll give plenty of grist to the rumor mill—and that is the last thing you need in the middle of a change effort. Your best bet here is to own the process by orchestrating the communication and getting the message out the way you want it delivered. This is the way to be sure that any folks who may want to detract from your message never have the chance to derail your plan.

Ask for feedback regularly. You have the goal in mind and a process to drive the change—but there will be many changes to the plan along the way. Hardly ever does a major change effort happen without hiccups and a need to readjust the strategy a bit. Think of it this way—if you are driving from Chicago to Orlando, you have a route planned but you won't know about last minute road closures, traffic accidents, and gridlock. You have a pretty good idea that things like this could happen and that you could run into these issues but the specifics won't be known until you run upon them. The same is true with change. You certainly know there will be obstacles but whom and what they might be will be invisible until they occur. Just like the car trip analogy, you probably have a good idea of potential choke points just like you know you might hit traffic in Atlanta, but you'll deal with it when you get there. So it's important not to get bogged down with what could go wrong, but at the same time be ready to adjust and have a backup plan in mind.

When you speak to your team throughout the change effort to be sure that you are eliciting feedback and really listening. There will be those who complain because folks struggle with change and there will be folks who have legitimate concerns. Take action on the relevant thoughts, but also give time to those who just need some time on the couch to get comfortable with the change. Folks get on board at different speeds; just know that sooner rather than later you need to have everyone in lock step.

Reward and celebrate successes and give away credit freely: There is nothing better than feeling good about a job well done. We have discussed praise throughout this book and it is just as important during change. Trust me, if you ask your team to execute this fantastic change for your Customers and business then fail to recognize their successes, you'll have a hard time getting them to help you again. Remember as the Leader you win when the change works—so give away the praise to those who made the change happen. You're not an individual contributor who rebranded the web site, the marketing pieces, the training program, but rather the person whose vision set the path. Energize your team by making sure they feel appreciated and that others in the organization know about their success and everyone comes out a winner.

Scale the knowledge: When you lead a change effort it could be something that impacts your department or a large organization. The good news is that you will learn lessons that you can use on a larger scale later. The ask here is to be sure that you not only share what you learn with your team but with your network to be sure everyone can learn. Too often in the past it was thought that keeping this kind of knowledge to yourself would make you more valuable and serve as a source of power. That is old school thinking that weak leaders lean on due to lack of self-confidence. The true measure of a great leader is the openness to share what is learned with everyone for the good of the organization. The best part about this is that it makes you seen as a source of great information who knows how to make the most of those great pearls you discover along the change highway. The next time folks need a change agent or someone who knows how to parlay learning into results chances are it will be you that they call.

Follow up consistently to be sure that the team doesn't revert back to old habits: Some change is sticky by nature—maybe a new computer program to book hotel stays or a new Point of Sale System for checking out Customers. Others may be procedural items such as how to make a chicken pot pie or clean a carpet. In most cases, something as cut and dry as a new computer program will stick because there isn't much wiggle room there. Things that have latitude—that is to say, procedures that require compliance have a tendency to backslide if they aren't fully baked into the culture, trained, monitored, and enforced. Folks are apt to want to revert back to a way that is familiar and in their minds easier unless they know that you are not willing to budge on your standards. Customer service is one of those things that are about doing things per the standards, which means that places it firmly in the second category. Folks can choose to do or not to do it—and you must do everything you can to make sure that folks stay on the path. If you don't, then you will never get the level of service for your Customers that you seek.

Here are a few key points that you will want to consider as you plot your organizations execution for the future. The key is to never get too comfortable with what is working today, but to keep looking at what will work better tomorrow.

Mobile will Continue to be Key: As the Millennials control a larger portion of the total spend in the marketplace, this is one key area where they demand a nod. The need for an online storefront has gone from a point of differentiation to price of entry. Today's Customers are more comfortable with self-service than ever before, so don't deprive them of the opportunity to make reservations, order, and pay online. They are even willing (and eager) to complete returns and fill out comment cards on the go. Just make sure that your online presence is as user friendly on mobile as it is on a desktop. I can tell you that there are still many organizations that haven't moved to a format that does well on all platforms.

Quick Responses are the Expectation: Most organizations are pretty good at responding to Customer comments. Granted there are still some airlines and hotels that struggle here, but generally everyone has a social media feed along with the standard email and web site. So with those in place, the way to get ahead is to make sure that someone is actually watching those feeds. Take the time to respond back quickly and not just with a "Please Call Us" response. If they wanted to call, they would have. Get comfortable with responding back right there in the feed or with a Direct Message (or DM). Many still struggle here, so this arena is ripe to be owned.

Consistency Continues to Win: The big WOWs are so much fun. They make everyone feel warm and fuzzy, but those feelings fade quickly. Keep in mind that consistency builds loyalty in a way that a few huge interactions won't. So this is where key scripting, great training, and tight processes will help you win. If you don't take the time to be sure that your team understands the basics of great service along with having the tools to deliver, you'll be way behind here. The good news is that if you can make the same cheeseburger or complete the same transaction with consistent success, you'll see your Customers returning over and over again. The businesses that struggle are those who deliver an A+ product one day and a D- the next.

Personalized Service is the Norm: Folks love things that are just for them. The Have-It-Your-Way mentality is here to stay. This could mean shoes and clothing ordered and made on demand, it could be entrees customized by diners when they are ordered, or it could be getting just the features they want in their computers. This will continue to be an important service touch point for businesses and will only continue to become more prevalent. Hotels will continue to have different options available in their rooms, restaurants will have to be ready for dietary challenges and taste preferences, and retailers will continue to drive for personalized service. The key take-a-way here is that you must find a way to not be seen as cookie cutter. How can you make each service interaction feel as though it was just for that Customer and that you understand that they are a constituency of one that deserves your special attention? Finding a way to answer that question and execute on those on values can certainly make you successful in the New Year.

Online Reviews Rule: Although comments on Yelp, Facebook, and Twitter are a way of life, some folks seem way too comfortable dismissing them. They matter. They are important. And they can impact your business. Take the time to read your own online press and take action to correct any miscues you may discover. Don't let them run your life, but be aware that they are out there. This is also a great reason to keep your social media feed relevant and that you drive traffic there—better to have Customers reach out to you on a channel you control rather than one you don't. So while this may not be earth shattering, no review of 2015 would be complete without acknowledging this reality.

Base Expectations = Delight: We are continuing to see a divergence in Customer Service. There really is no middle ground. . . Either businesses are rocking the house with amazing service that delights and surprises or they couldn't care less. Believe it or not, as the year goes along, those who can deliver on the base of a strong welcome and polite service will continue to be given credit for being amazing. Now those who knock it out of the yard will certainly be beloved beyond all others, but just hitting the base expectations will be rewarded as well.

Remember through it all that change is rarely easy and sometimes scary. To you it may seem like the most logical progression in the world and if you are working to integrate change that benefits your Customer experience, your heart is definitely in the right place. Just don't forget to put yourself in your team's shoes and understand that you will have to exercise all of your Leadership muscle to complete the change. It's definitely worth the effort, but you'll need to follow the steps listed above to give yourself the best chance of success.

Above all, remember that if you walk your team through the process and work with them in a kind but resolute manner, you'll see improvement that will help you drive that great Customer experience.

CHAPTER 16
Owning The Service

*"The only way to move forward and drive great
service is to own it—every minute of every day!"*

Tony Johnson

The best way to get started is just to do it. We have covered a
lot of ground in these pages and I am so thankful that you stayed
with me as you commit to deliver that great service. I have great
confidence that you will take these ideas and thoughts, and put
them to great use for your Customers. I applaud the commitment
you are showing to amazing service and I thank you for taking this
journey with me.

Remember that great service means doing the right things for
your Customers but at the same time driving revenue for your
business. For the most part we are all looking to drive revenue
and profit in today's competitive market—and even if you are not
a for-profit organization, making sure you drive a great experience
is just as crucial. So please be sure to keep in mind the end goal of
great service: a fantastic Customer experience that drives profitable
growth.

The good news is that no one sets out to deliver bad service
and be unprofitable—but some do get lost along the way or don't
realize how tough it is to execute. Don't beat yourself up if you
haven't been doing a great job and don't fret about what may have
gone wrong in the past.

This is the chance for a new beginning. This is your time to
embrace the need to show your Customers the love, develop your
teams, and plot a new course for loyalty.

My advice to you is to take some time to plan and script your next moves. Meet with your leadership team, your direct supervisor, and your staff to discuss what to do next. You have to remember that you can't do it alone and you can't do it overnight. If you try to do either of those things then you are setting yourself up for failure. As we discussed in the previous chapter, you will need to be clear but decisive in your mission. That doesn't mean that you shouldn't listen if someone has a great thought, and of course you have to integrate this into your larger organization mission, but put your faith in the Customer service points we have discussed throughout this book.

Here are some thoughts you should consider:

- How is my training and onboarding?
- Who will be the key team members in this quest? Bring them in early and create champions to further the cause of great service. You can't do it alone.
- Are there small, quick moves that will make a big impact?
- How will you touch the hearts of your team to drive service improvement?
- How is your Customer service (yes, you personally)? Are you setting the example you want to see in your team?
- Do you have the right leadership team in place to improve Customer service?
- How will you reward and celebrate your upcoming successes?
- What exactly does great service look like in the context of your organization?
- What benefits will you realize by implementing this great service—and how will you articulate these benefits to your team?

This is your call to action. You have to get amped up about great service—simply put, you have to want it. There is no magic bullet to make your team fall in line and deliver. It takes constant management each minute of each shift to deliver great service to your Customers.

This is one of those times when the solution is easy to understand but takes real effort to execute. You know as a Leader what makes up great service. That is what has made you successful. But your team needs you to show those examples every day and hold them accountable.

Remember that your team needs your guidance and reinforcement. Too often change efforts take on a flavor-of-the-month feel that does little more than encourage folks to wait it out until the policy changes. When that kind of thinking takes hold, you will never get the buy in you need from the front lines to drive great service. Fortunately, most teams are hungry for that leadership that inspires and promises big things. So feel confident in setting this course toward great Customer service.

I have waited until now to discuss the huge WOW! We all know they are important but I didn't want to take away from the commitment to the consistent service that most folks skimp on.

There is magic to be had out there—and there are countless stories out there that tell the story. I want to discuss the magic of NORAD. Yes, that's right: NORAD. In 1955, a Sears Department Store advertisement in Colorado published the wrong phone number for a line to call and talk to Santa. Famously, the Colonel on duty instructed his staff to give Santa's "current location" to the children calling in. Now he could have just hung up or dismissed the children, but he didn't. Chances are he wasn't all that happy about the calls—but he stepped up and delivered. Today, this program uses over a thousand volunteers to staff the phones and this has become famous around the world with over 100,000 callers between Christmas Eve and Christmas Day. This is such a great example of going the extra mile and it shows that amazing service can come from anyone at any time if he or she just has the will to make it happen.

There are famous stories out there—a notable department store that took back a set of defective tires, when they don't carry them in store. An online retailer donated a huge order of shoes to those serving in the military when they got a large order wrong. And airline flight attendants who sing, dance, and tell fantastic jokes. All of these magic moments can help to deepen the relationship between you and your Customers—and they are important.

So think about those things that can drive magic. Make sure your team understands what they are empowered to provide and script the moves. They need a little latitude to be creative within those parameters and you can't lose your mind if they occasionally go too far. Trust me when I tell you that if you are looking for the occasional WOW, you will have someone who will overstep. Use it as a coaching moment but don't make them eat it.

But what does that look like? It could be a complimentary dessert for a regular restaurant diner. It could be commenting on someone's birthday and singing when they enter the bank. It could also be a complimentary chocolate selection left in the room of a regular hotel Guest. There are a multitude of ways you can go the extra step for your Customer, just never lose sight of the consistency that allows you to make those WOWs a reality. But embrace them. Love them. Celebrate them. And be sure that you are using them to drive word of mouth.

Make sure your team is well trained, understands the mission, and knows that you are passionately committed to consistently great service that always pushes for the amazing. Be honest with them about the importance of delivering the complete Customer experience—including a candid check in on where you currently stand. Start by establishing where you are strong and where improvement is needed and don't let anything push you off message. Belief in yourself and the need for great service will be contagious as you inspire your team to put the Customer at the center of everything you do.

But most importantly, get excited about serving your Customers and let you inner joy help inspire your team.

Trust me, it will!

Commit To Win!

*"Put the Customer at the center of what
you do. Only then can you win!"*

Tony Johnson

I want to thank you again for taking this journey with me. I know your time is valuable and a finite resource that is not to be wasted.

That you saw the value in this message means a lot to me and I know that you are off to amazing things. Only the best take the time to improve their leadership and only the very best put that development focus squarely on their Customers.

So much is possible when you selflessly put the Customer first and commit to do nothing short of delight them. Meet their expectations and watch your relationships flourish and grow. This will also give you the framework to better lead your teams to put their Customers at the center of their world.

Don't forget to reach out if I can be of any additional assistance to you. To be great you must first embrace the fact that you can't know everything and that asking for help is not a sign of weakness. That is a lesson that it took me far too long to learn and once I embraced it my career took a whole different turn.

You can always find me for extra Customer Service Magic and MOTIVATION at:

www.TheTonyJohnson.com
Feel free to reach out to me or my assistant directly:
Tony@TheTonyJohnson.com
Melissa@TheTonyJohnson.com

I am also available to speak to your group or organization. If you need a high energy trainer for your next event or conference, reach out directly at:

Info@TheTonyJohnson.com

Dates are booking fast, so please call TODAY to add **Motivation, Customer Focus,** and **High Energy** to your Event!

Tony Johnson

Made in the USA
Columbia, SC
17 October 2020

22798330R00075